Divine Bud:
Testimonies of God's
Intervention

Philip Mutaka

Langaa Research & Publishing CIG
Mankon, Bamenda

Publisher
Langaa RPCIG
Langaa Research & Publishing Common Initiative Group
P.O. Box 902 Mankon
Bamenda
North West Region
Cameroon
Langaagrp@gmail.com
www.langaa-rpcig.net

Distributed in and outside N. America by African Books Collective
orders@africanbookscollective.com
www.africanbookcollective.com

ISBN: 9956-727-58-X

© Philip Mutaka 2012

Table of Contents

iv

Foreword

"Before we go to bed, let us pray," said Jacky.

During the whole evening of May 6, 2009, Jacky, Georgina, Nadine, and Eric have been selecting the items that Georgina and Jacky would bring to Ghana for their stay in preparation to Georgina's surgical operation. Everything was ready. They will be traveling tomorrow.

For a long time, all the family had been praying for Georgina's surgical operation. She was born with a congenital scoliosis, and this single handicap had affected the family in various respects. Our most fervent prayer had always been that God heed our prayers. I will recount the different problems we encountered in this request for God's intervention in favor of Georgina later in this novel. I have just used the term novel, but, as my readers will notice, it is not really a novel. It is based on reality. What makes it a novel is the organization of the events. But the stories are factual.

I was in the sitting room when I heard Jacky inviting the children to pray. For a long time, I had ceased praying with the family. It is not that I did not like to pray. It is just that I had decided that it was far better for me to stop praying with the family because I never wanted my children to believe that, even if you persevere in your prayers, God may not answer them. I have always believed that my whole existence would be shattered if my children were to think that I am a liar when I always tell them that, somehow, God will answer our prayers and that Georgina will get operated somehow. Despite the various efforts we had made to have her operated mostly in the States, we usually obtained negative responses. The Shriners Hospital for children in Boston, Massachusetts, which was our first serious hope, turned us down because they said that the operation would have to take place in three phases. Contrary to the predictions of the surgical doctor who acted as Georgina's local Cameroonian doctor, it could not be done once and Georgina could not simply stay in the States for a period of three months. Besides, as parents, we would have to obtain a visa and have her travel to the States. Nothing could be done as long as she stayed here in Africa.

Another Shriners Hospital of Philadelphia simply turned us down because they said that, in order to envisage her operation, she simply has to be in the States. As long as she is in Africa, they were not going to study her dossier. However, they are the ones who put us into contact with the Focos team, a medical organization which also makes seasonal stays in Ghana to do orthopedic operations. Dr. Boachie Adjei, its doctor, is Ghanaian living and working in the States. To alleviate the difficulties for African children who could not afford traveling to the States, his organization usually asks the patients to go to Ghana and meet him there. The patients were to get to Accra, Ghana, two to three weeks before his arrival. For this year, he was going to come on May 23, 2009 and that is why Georgina was to arrive there by the beginning of May.

As I heard Jacky inviting children to pray together, I also joined them. Nadine was in bed. Georgina was kneeling before the bed. Eric was standing and I came to stand by the door of Georgina's room where the prayers were to be conducted.

It is Jackie who conducted the prayer. Among the prayers, there was the Lord's prayer, that is, "Our father who art in heaven," followed by Hail Mary and a Glory be to the Father. After that, Jackie started addressing her personal prayers to

God from the bottom of her heart. For me who heard it, it was very emotional. One sensed how grateful she was to God for allowing the arrival of this day when she would finally travel with her daughter to have her operated.

"Lord God, we just want to thank you for always taking care of us. For a long time, we have always prayed that this day may come, that is, that Georgina be given a chance to be operated on for her backbone problem. We simply want to thank you in our hearts, and I pray that you protect us during the travel to Ghana and during the whole stay in Ghana. I pray that you always be with the doctor who will operate on Georgina, that you be the one guiding all this operation. I also pray that you continue to look at the rest of my family that will stay here during our absence. You also know that I left my own mother in Butembo in a convalescence state. I pray that you continue to look after her and have pity on her and make her recover. I pray all this in the name of Jesus."

A short silence intervened. In fact, two weeks earlier, Jacky was in Butembo, the capital city of the Nande, her ethnic community. She had gone there hurriedly because her mother called for her. She thought she was getting to the end of her life and wanted to see her children around her before she departs from this world. Fortunately, by the time Jacky returned, she was doing better. In fact, she was no longer at the hospital. She was getting treatment from a traditional herbalist because it had been determined that she had been poisoned. Western medication was not efficient to treat the sequels of this kind of poisoning. As a consequence of that poisoning, her mother decided to no longer return to her native village because she knew that she was poisoned by a neighbor and she no longer wanted to put her life in jeopardy. In a sense, Jacky's prayers reflected the sum of urgent worries she had and that she entrusted to God because she knew that he was the ultimate savior who alone would be able to look after Georgina, her own sick mother, and her family that she would temporarily leave in Cameroon without a mother. After the short silence, I heard Georgina praying.

"Lord God, I want to thank you for finally heeding our prayers. For a long time, we have always prayed you so that I might get a chance to get operated. You have now answered this prayer as I will be traveling to Ghana tomorrow. I pray that you always stay with us, that you protect us during the travel, that you bless the doctor who will operate on me. I ask you all this in the name of Jesus."

"Amen," we all answered as we were happy with the prayer.

Soon after Georgina ended her prayer, Nadine also prayed. The quintessence of her prayer was also to thank God for having finally answered our prayer. I must confess that I always admired Nadine. Sometimes, I thought Nadine is the pastor of the family. Just like Georgina. They knew how to pray, to address themselves to God with all their trust in him. As you heard them, you could not doubt that God must heed their prayers. It is amazing the way they have mastered personal prayers that they address to God. As children that have grown as Catholics, they were expected to know the recitation prayers. However, they must have learned from their parents who definitely admired the way Protestants pray. Their prayers are much more personal, more genuine. They are not mere recitations. One feels that the praying person is really addressing himself to God. Nadine and Georgina had learned that and this was truly admirable.

After the prayers, we bid good night to one another and, as usual, we ended this "good night" with "God bless you."

Chapter 1

Shattered hope

On May 7, 2009, I drove Jackie and Georgina to the bus station early in the morning. Their plane was to leave Duala in the afternoon. So they had to arrive in Duala around 10: am. Eric and Nadine also boarded the car. We all wanted to see Georgina and Mommy travel safely to the bus and they would go to Duala and later on fly to Ghana. Georgina had borrowed my bag that I had used in the past to travel to Brazil. This was now her own bag. As they left, our hope was that they would come back with Georgina in a new body. We were full of hope as we saw her boarding the bus and leaving for Duala with her mom.

From the telephone calls and the SMS messages we usually got from them in Ghana, Georgina truly socialized perfectly with other kids. She realized that other kids were even worse than her. Everybody liked her.

On the eve of her operation, she did express her fear. This was normal. The doctor had concluded that he could not do a deep operation because it would be dangerous. She would probably lose a lot of blood and there was a risk that she be confined to bed for a long time. The doctor was only going to correct the deformities.

Actually, during the period that preceded the arrival of Dr. Boachie in Accra, Georgina did a lot of lab tests. Some of them were expensive. Fortunately, we did not have to pay for them. They were covered by the deposit that we had paid as a prerequisite for her treatment by the Focos team. As Jackie later told me, the local anesthetist did express openly his worries that her operation would be very difficult as he noticed that her lungs were not well developed. To him, the operation would last some eight hours and he was not sure that Georgina's lungs would support such a long time. Yet, when Dr. Boachie examined her case, he did not see that as a problem. Or, if he did, he did not mention it. What he simply decided is that he was going to make corrections of her spine. He thus instructed the nurses to put a crown on Georgina's head. I have only seen that crown in a picture as Georgina decided to put it on her mom's mobile telephone. As Jackie told me, this crown made her very uncomfortable because she had to sleep with it. On the eve of the operation, she asked Jackie what she thought of her condition as she said that she was somehow afraid. She even said that she hopes that the doctors know that her breathing is not that normal. Although she had discovered that the deformities of some of the other children were worse than hers, she observed that their breathing remained nonetheless normal. Hers was not. She told Jackie that she hoped that the doctor knows about it.

About her discomfort with the crown, her mom told her that she simply has to bear it for that one day. After all we have been praying for the arrival of this day that she finally gets operated, and it behooved her to support it. She told her about the suffering of Jesus Christ's Passion, that is, during the last days of his life. This seemed to soothe her a lot. She knew that she was thus experiencing, with that crown, the kind of suffering that the Lord Jesus Christ had gone through with his thorny crown. At a certain time, she even found that crown was efficient because, for the first time, as she bent, she was able to touch her toes, something that she had always been incapable of doing before.

2

On the day of her operation, she woke up as usual. Somehow, when they came to look for her, Jackie was not in the room. She simply learned that the Focos team had come to get her and brought her to the operating ward. Georgina thus went to the operation room, full of hope. That was the d-day. In the morning, I had written to some of my friends to pray for her. I sent them SMS messages as I knew they were very close to God. One is a pastor. The other is a friend of mine living in the States. No one responded. By 2 o'clock, I got a call from Jackie. I wondered why she would call so early. I knew that the operation would take a long time and I was only expecting to hear from her in the evening. I knew that this would be the beginning of a new life. We would have to adjust to Georgina's confinement in bed while she would be recovering from her surgical operation. But lo! What Jacky told me was: "Georgina is no more." What a shock. It was a great setback. What we had believed to be the epitome of God's intervention in Georgina's life was this sad news. I had to find a way to relay it to Arlette, her big sister. I was to do it. I also had to tell other people. Jackie called a second time and told me that the doctor wanted to talk to me. He explained how Georgina died. It was just at the beginning of the whole set up for the operation. The operation had not even started. They introduced a tube in her mouth. As her neck was no longer straight, the tube could not be inserted. It suffocated her. In no time, Georgina was dead.

The question is: did God really answer our prayers? If I said yes, it would be like cheating. We did not obtain what we wanted. It was in fact the opposite of what all of us were expecting. It is true that, in my case, I knew that today would be the beginning of a different life. I was worried that Georgina will have to undergo a period of suffering while she is recovering from her operation. I never imagined how they would even straighten her back. It is true that the doctor had already decided that he would not do a deep operation. He would simply correct the scoliosis. Even there, there would be internal wounds. Maybe, she would have to stay in bed for a long time. I knew it would be very painful for me, as her father, to live her own suffering.

All this was annihilated. She was dead. I said to myself that God did not want her to suffer. That is why she died without even suffering. She did not know that she would die. Her spirit surely decided to go back to God. You might laugh, but I think it is true. Some days later, as I sent an email message to Dr. Boachie about the obituary notes I had written about Georgina, saying that she is a saint, he also reacted that Georgina went back to God with her body unscathed. No one scarred it.

My readers will find me a bit strange. No single tear has dropped from my eyes. But I have sometimes suffered internally because of the separation. I still see her when she goes to school, a small girl, very polite. Sometimes she would look back and she saw me. She knew that I cared for her. On Sundays, we always ate her preferred food. We still eat her preferred dish on Sundays, and it always reminds us of her absence. It still makes us suffer. I am nonetheless released because my wife and Nadine still refer to her as if she was still present. I know that, for other people, pronouncing the name of a dead person may be painful. It is not in our case. What I have only observed is that Jackie wanted me to hang her picture at a place in the living room that does not immediately attract our look.

Why have I never cried? In my mind, Georgina is with God. Georgina is a saint. I know how she left. I know that

4

she was close to God. I know that, in the Catholic religion, to be recognized as a saint, there is a whole administrative process. But, why would I not believe that Georgina is a saint? If she is not, then I am a liar when I confess that I am Christian. As I look back to her life, I do not remember something that would have condemned her. Of course, as a human being, she was not perfect. Sometimes, she would tease her younger sister Nadine or scold her brother Eric. There are some Sundays that she was too busy with her school work and that she would not go to church. This was rare though. But, during all this period when we knew that she would go to Ghana for the operation, she was a saint. I knew it whenever I would go to her room and pray with them.

Here is the obituary note I wrote on her.

What can I say about Georgina Mutaka?
Her life:
She was born in Yaounde on April 21, 1993 at the CHU Hospital. Her nationality: Congolese (DRC).

She was born with a congenital scoliosis. In a sense, she has always been very special. As a matter of fact, for her baptism, her father got special permission from Mgr Jean Zoa so that her godparents for this baptism be a protestant couple, notably, the couple of Pastor Kamate Basolene. However, at the actual mass at Mont Febe, it was a Catholic priest, Father Faustin, who acted as her godfather. As for the choice of her name: we had met a priest in the States who, to us, was the symbol of holiness. He was a humble man but who knew how to show his holiness through simple every day acts. He was Jackie's boss. He was the chief priest of the Catholic parish that was attached to the University of

Southern California, Los Angeles. It is in remembrance of Father George Luznicky that Georgina got her name. We are happy to notice that her life has been able to touch the hearts of so many people who have sent us their testimonies of compassion when she died. Thank you to all her classmates, thank you to the children of the Catholic doctrine at Christ-Roi of Tsinga, thank you the religious nuns and the catechists of Tsinga for your messages, thanks to all of you who have sent us your sympathy testimonies. Thank you Prof. Sow and your family: it is Khadija, your daughter who was her very first friend in this world.

To a certain extent, Georgina had shaped the life of her family. Our prayer, since she was born, had always been that her scoliosis be corrected. Her dossier was first sent to UCLA when she was still a baby. Then the medical doctors in Yaounde proposed her evacuation to France. Doctoral students from the University of Torino, Italy, brought her dossier to Italy. In the States, her dossier has been examined by two Shriners hospitals at Massachusetts and Philadelphia. Her dossier is also at the Vatican. The responses that we usually received were that, either the operation would be too expensive, more than 300,000 US dollars in Italy; for the States, the operation was to take place in three phases and they would not consider operating on her as long as she is still in Africa. Finally, Shriners Hospital of Philadelphia suggested that Focos which had an antenna in Ghana take up her case. It is thus in Ghana that she went for this surgical operation three weeks ago. Georgina has just died in Accra on May 28, 2009, the day when she was scheduled to get her surgical operation. Very probably, her remains will be buried in Ghana.

Here is the text that accompanied her picture:

Georgina,

You know what! Your numerous friends have been crying because you left them. Beginning by Nadine, Eric, and your school mates, Pierrette, Valerie, Nanou, Arlette, Rosine, Colette, Hardie, even adults like Tantine Louise, Aude, Judith, Pauline, Marie, and Georgina. Maman Chantal says that you are now an angel in heaven. So many people love you. Some promised to request masses in your honor in Paris, Bukavu, Butembo, and of course, we will do one here in Yaounde when Mommy returns from Ghana. Bye. You will always be in our hearts.

Here is the text that I sent to some of you to announce Georgina's passing away.

Subject: Bye Georgina

Arlette,

Today (i.e., May 28, 2009) was the d day. But the Lord God decided to call back Georgina to HIM.

As the doctor was trying to introduce something in her throat, because her spine was already crooked, she did not resist. She immediately died. Jacky has just called me and she was still in the hospital.

As Christians, we have to accept the fact. The positive thing about it is that Georgina dies, I would say, as a saint. The day before they traveled to Ghana, Jackie, Nadine, and Georgina each prayed. And I admired their prayers. They are able to talk to the Lord God. Georgina was so grateful that the Lord has finally answered our prayers and that she will thus get operated. I do not think she has suffered before dying. She is preceding us in heaven. As Christians, I do not

7

see why she would not go to heaven, near her God who has called her back.

For the time being, I do not know whether her body will be sent back here to Cameroon.

Thank you everyone of you who had supported us in your prayers. The ways of the Lord are not always easy to understand. The fact is that she is now dead. May her soul rest in peace and return peacefully to our Lord who created us and who alone knows our fate here on earth.

Best.

Philip

By way of concluding this obituary note, here is a message that conveys the pain of separation:

My dear brother Mutaka,

As I am writing this note, I really have a great quantity of tears flowing from my eyes. Mary had just announced this bad news to me while crying. She was unable to reach the end of her news. Yes, she has gone to heaven to her father who wanted to spare her the sufferings of the planet Earth. We would have preferred that she remains in our midst in her state. Man proposes but God takes the ultimate decision. What you have done, you did it out of sheer love that parents have for their children. You did your duty; you do not have to worry about that. Be courageous, we are with you in this pain; your suffering is also ours. May the soil of our ancestors be light to her and that the Lord our God welcome her in heaven. We pray this with our utmost faith.

Courage.

Nduire Kakungu Cardinal.

Other people have insisted that she is a saint. If you see the testimonies that came from people we did not even know, you would readily accept that she is truly a saint. She had touched the hearts of so many people, such as her school mates and elderly women in our quarter. I remember one coming to tell us that Georgina never passed without greeting her. Another came to tell us that she sometimes rested at her place while coming from school. She was very much attached to her. Maman Chantal, our landlady who was actually living in Paris, kept telling us that she is a saint, that she is an angel. She insisted that we could not even imagine her as being in the purgatory. She must have gone straight to the paradise. Mrs Babang also came to pray with us, and she convinced us that she is a saint. To me, Georgina is a saint. But I must reveal something. Since she was my daughter, I felt that, in her sainthood, she no longer belongs to my nuclear family. She belongs to the community of saints in heaven as we, Catholics and Protestants believe about what happens to the soul upon one's death. Yet, I told myself that she should be able to present my problems to God because she knew them. I asked her a favor. I wanted her to manifest herself and tell me where she is.

I slept. I somehow knew that she would manifest herself. There are times I woke up and did not see her manifesting herself. At a certain time, while I was asleep, she came to reassure us. She was smiling. She wanted to also reassure her mom. But her mom was not sure because she knew that she was dead. I had a very nice interaction with her. She left me with very good impressions. I have been including her among the saints in heaven who can intervene for us. Georgina, you are a saint. I know it. It is something that one cannot explain,

9

but in your case, you are. You are part of the concept of the "divine bud" that I will hopefully explain later on in this book. It is a concept that is closely related to what Jesus said, I guess, to the Pharisees: be like small children. He knew that small children are innocent, that they are the true embodiment of sainthood on earth, and possibly in heaven. You have died while preserving your sainthood and your positive impact on people who have known you is a testimony to this. It is sainthood that goes beyond Christians. It also touches other faiths as will be found in a testimony of a Buddhist I plan to include in this book in one of the last chapters. You can now understand why I have never cried. The reason is because I know that it is God who called you back to Him.

Chapter 2

Georgina's Short Life

The story of Georgina is a long one. She was conceived in the States, more precisely, at Santa Cruz, in northern California. We had just spent one academic year there after we had left Los Angeles where I had been a student at USC. Because I was a student, I never bothered about the necessity of having a second child. We had one child, Arlette, and I was wholly satisfied with her. What I never knew is that women are much more maternal. My wife always wanted to have a child while we were in the States. I think it had been her secret because she knew that I would probably oppose it as I was a student and would not have money to support a baby. When Georgina was conceived, it was at a time when I came back from England for a job interview. I had left my family for almost one month because I was blocked in Great Britain. When I came back, I think that we did not have time to check my wife's menstruation. For Jackie who always wanted to become pregnant, this was good news. To her, a single child was not sufficient. She is African.

As we came to Cameroon, we stayed at SIL. That is where the first problem with Georgina, still in her mom's womb, started. Jackie saw blood although she knew that she was pregnant. She became really crazy. She could not lose her child. An American lady who works at SIL brought us hurriedly to CHU. She was examined, and fortunately, the child was saved. This pregnancy left a deep scar in me. It showed how different I was from my wife. Maybe, men are really different from women. Women carry children in their womb, and the idea of losing a child is so traumatic to them. Jackie became really crazy. I did not support her. I remember, even my daughter Arlette was to bring me back to reason. She saw the serious disagreement with my wife. I never thought that the blood she had discovered on her during her pregnancy was that dangerous. For my wife, it was dangerous. That was the end of the story.

Later on, she followed the regular consultations. This is again where I saw that Cameroon is different from the States. The Cameroonian doctor would prescribe us something like 12 different medications. I asked him why he was doing that. He was shocked. He could not understand why a patient would question him. He did not know that I was coming from the States. I told him so. I told him that I had to know why medication would be given to my wife. Anyway, I never bought those medications. I suspected that it was a way for these doctors to simply make money. Twelve different medications! That was not right.

The day Georgina was born, at first, we thought she was normal. But somehow, she was crooked. Unfortunately, the doctor immediately diagnosed her scoliosis. She was missing 6 ribs. There was a French doctor at the hospital. He prescribed her a corset. But it never did anything positive.

Another doctor from the States happened to be here in Yaounde on a visit as we were staying with her daughter. She took Georgina's pictures along those of us, her parents, and she brought the dossier to UCLA. She never got back to us.

We started visiting various doctors. Georgina was handicapped. We usually brought her to Etoug-ebe. Some doctors said that her scoliosis could be straightened when she is 18 years old. Another doctor told us that her case was difficult. He showed us pictures of children who were like her. Her scoliosis was a very rare case. But it happened. He explained that, as she grows up, she will be having problems of breathing and that she will develop a serious hump. This doctor described to us the worst scenario that would happen to Georgina. As parents, my wife and I did not believe it. I knew that she would be ok. She was not exactly ok. But she grew up in a normal way. Now that she is dead, I must say that we have enjoyed having her for 16 years. She sometimes had breathing problems. Mommy used to massage her. This had become part of our regular life.

We presented her dossier to several places. Two Italian anthropology students from the University of Torino, Ivo and Sylvia, together with their professor and a best friend of mine, Professor Francesco Remotti, are the ones who first remarked her handicap and asked us to make a dossier on her that they would bring to Italy. They were ready to raise money in their country in order to have Georgina operated. After several months, they informed us that the operation would be too expensive: at least 300,000 US dollars in Italy. A Cameroonian doctor tried to put us in contact with a French doctor. But he said we have to give him at least 10 million francs. And my salary at that time was only 426 000 CFA francs. There is another doctor who was serious and who was really concerned. He recommended her to his own professor in France. But again, nothing ever succeeded. That is how we turned to the States. We tried the Shriners Hospitals that a very dear friend of mine, Dr. Pat Schneider, had discovered that their doctors could operate on Georgina for free. All this time, we had been praying. But nothing worked. We were turned down because, in order for Georgina to be operated, she had to be in the States.

13

My whole life and that of our family was organized around Georgina. I was thinking seriously of going back to the States. This is also an opportunity for me to reveal why I was once conned.

As people say, only God and Satan have access to our thoughts. Unfortunately Satan knew that I trusted God and that I wanted Georgina to get operated. We saw lottery stuff on internet. I examined it because I was told that I had won that lottery. I thought that someone had introduced my name. Curiously enough, I heard my daughter Nadine say that we would be going to the States. No one ever told her that we would go to the States. I interpreted this as an answer from God. This was not God. This was Satan's work. I could not see it. At first, they took 350,000 francs from me. Then they succeeded to take 1,500,000 CFA francs, that is, the equivalent of three thousand US dollars from me. I thought it was worth it if Georgina can get to the States and be operated. Besides, this was money that I had earned in the States while I was a student and subsequently as an administrative staff in my home university, that is, the University of Southern California, and one year as an assistant teacher in the department of linguistics at the University of California at Santa Cruz.

When it was found out that Georgina could be operated in Ghana, we were happy. The problem of money was raised. At first, we were told that it would be around 3000 dollars. Then they changed it to 5000 dollars, then 6000 dollars. At a certain time, I had my daughter call them from the States. They then made it 25000 dollars. I told them that I could not pay that money because I was merely a University teacher working in Africa. Finally, we agreed on 6000 dollars. In addition, I had to pay airplane tickets and everything else. I have paid around 5 million francs. I have never complained. I thought the University could reimburse me since I was not expected to get all that money from my savings for my work in Cameroon. My salary is relatively low. But with Georgina's death, I could no longer file such a claim. I reread the contract I had signed with the University of Yaounde, which is my employer; they never stated that they could help me in case a member of my family would become sick or die. That is the bad thing about working in our African countries. Especially foreigners like me. But, what can I say? They are not the ones who made my government irresponsible and that we could not be encouraged to work in our own countries. This is not the point anyway.

The good thing is that I always believed that God was with me. I did not have problems for obtaining the 6000 dollars plus all the money for the various tickets I have had to pay for Georgina, Jacky, and later on Arlette as she had to come and join Jacky in Ghana when she learned that Georgina passed away. Sometimes, I wonder how I succeed to manage the money that I get when I consider my expenses and my net salary. But money has never been a problem. The reason may be that I do not spend money unnecessarily. And yet, I do spend a lot of money on my publications for example. Again, I must say that money has never been a problem. In fact, nothing has ever been a serious problem for us. I may even include Georgina as never being a burden to my entire family. Although she was handicapped, she did not really consider herself as handicapped. Her mind was that of a very normal person. She nursed in her mind the project of becoming a doctor, or getting married and begetting children.

Maybe I should tell you something that made us happy, that is, her mom and me. One day, while she was still in the primary school, she came to tell us that she was elected by some boys as one of the most beautiful girls in her class. This was good. Despite her scoliosis, she knew that people liked her nonetheless. She had friends, people I would qualify as true friends who never made her feel that she was handicapped. She was also friends with adults.

I remember, as part of Georgina's funerals a few days after her death, people requested masses on her behalf. In Bangui, they organized a special mass for her and people drank. My friends who organized that mass said that people who had never gone to church came to church on that day and then came to socialize with them by sharing food and drinks at their place. She was a blessing. In my mind, I had been preparing her return to Cameroon. And I wanted to thank God in a special way. I wanted to make people know that God hears our prayers. I thought I would write something about Focos to make them known. I even asked Georgina to be taking notes as I would use them to write the book. This passage in our father always touched me: "thy will be done on earth as it is in heaven." We always recite it. But do we believe that this can happen? In order for it to happen, we have to do something. I promised the Lord God that I would write a book in that sense. I know that I will not succeed. But if you can get a sense of that, then this novel is a success. I thought that the best way for me to do it is to write testimonies of God's intervention in our lives. This is the continuation of this book. I will write them as a novel. I will introduce some fiction in them. But all these stories are based on reality. I obtained them from my sociolinguistics students of the University of Yaounde 1. Let us now embark on the train of God's intervention in our lives before we get back to

Georgina as the central theme of this novel in the last chapters.

Chapter 3

Miraculous Recoveries

Why speak about God's intervention? If you look at the jungle, when some animals eat others, is it God who wanted it that way? Think about the malnourished children in Ethiopia that you might have seen on TV. Or the massacres in Rwanda, is it God who willed it? Think about the earthquakes and other natural catastrophes that kill thousands of people. Think mostly about the Muslims and the Christians. Most wars are done in the name of God. Do the Christians and the Muslims have the same God? If he is the true God, why doesn't he let us live in peace?

Take the Christians. There are among them several sects. Each sect says that its God is the true God. The Protestants sometimes do not consider Catholics as true Christians. Catholics sometimes suspect Protestants. For example, when talking about saints, only Catholics have saints. Does it mean that Protestants do not have saints? What about the Muslims? What about the Jews? So many people believe in God. So many people believe that they have been praying the right God.

Because we are in Cameroon, there is this problem of ancestors. The problem is mostly acute among the Bamileke who are very much attached to their traditions. They believe that the ancestors are the intermediary between them and God. Is this still the same God?

In what follows, I will be reporting stories written by my sociolinguistics students about what they believe has been God's intervention either in their lives or in the lives of their closest friends. Most of those stories will reveal that God is present among us. God is not an administrative God as the way he seems to be presented in the Catholic religion. For the Catholics, you have to abide by certain rules, created by theologians, in order to be heeded by God. Priests see themselves as closer to God, and they sometimes scare us if we disobey them because they think they are closer to God. In their minds, and as human beings, they know that they are not. God is God. We will never reduce him into what we want him to be. Although we had been praying him for Georgina, the way he responded was to call Georgina back to him. That was the very best decision. We do not know what would have happened to Georgina in terms of suffering or to us as her parents. God is almighty. He knows our past, our future and he knows what is best for us. Even when we are in the most difficult situations, God is never absent. But God wants us to call on him, to pray him in order for him to intervene in our lives. The stories you will hear are testimonies where God continues to make miracles just as he did during the time of Christ.

While I was pondering these issues in my mind, Margaret entered my office. She had heard that I had lost my daughter and she wanted to present her condolences. As I had told the students that I would prepare something to celebrate Georgina's recovery when she would return from Ghana, she reminded me that I do not have to feel sad. In fact, she was pleased to see that I was not that sad and that she could easily talk to me.

"You know what! I have always wanted to give you a personal testimony to show you that God does intervene in our lives. But, I have not had time to write it down. I have even started, but somehow, I succeeded to only write one page," said Margaret.

"I hope it is a real testimony, the kind of testimony that can really bring people to change their lives," I answered her.

"You will never find that kind of testimony. What do you mean the kind of testimony that can change people's lives?"

"Well, take our political authorities for example. Most of them claim that they are Christians. I see many of them at Mont Febe. I know some of them have even been asking 100 masses at Mont Febe for a relative of theirs who died. And yet, they are still the same people through whom a lot of injustice is perpetuated. I know that they are sometimes the agents of corruption. I have always wanted to find a way of making people repent and change their behavior to adapt it to the will of God voluntarily, that is, without having to be forced by external forces. Wouldn't this be great! Imagine the Talibans who seem to find pleasure in killing people were to stop causing havoc in the lives of their neighbors on their own will. This might make you laugh, but when I think about the recent election of the Iranian president, their spiritual chief as well as the newly elected president knew that they were accusing falsely the foreign countries of staging revolts in Iran. They knew it. The opposition also knew it as well. At a certain time, the spiritual chief had to relent on earlier declarations and state that he had not seen any evidence that the troubles were staged by foreign governments. He then accused the internal opposition. As he did it, he also knew that it was also wrong. He knew that the militia of the newly elected president had played some dirty tricks that contributed to the imposition of the president to be re-elected. Imagine that this spiritual leader as well as the Iranian president were to know that they do not have to justify themselves before men but before their God, don't you think that they would be more friendly towards the people they wrongly consider as their enemies, that is, the Jewish people or the Americans? In *Wish I had known*, I wrote a preface in which I tried to insist on the fact that, upon our death, we will have to account for our actions here on earth. Every one of us knows that he will die and that he will face his God. He will be asked to account for his actions on earth. I thought people would heed this message and start thinking about their purpose of living on earth. But, apparently, not many people have got the message."

"I see. But again, I know that you will not find this kind of testimony. Bear in your mind that the miracles God does in our everyday lives are things that may not be extraordinary. The simple fact that we live, that we are not knocked down by a car as we cross the road, the simple thing that we can breathe normally, all these are miracles. Yet what I am going to tell you is worth telling. I have two testimonies."

"Tell me those testimonies then. What is the first?"
"Well, I think it will be far better that I prepare it in writing. I promise to bring it to you in a few days. I will rather tell you about the second testimony that I have prepared in writing. It might be more convincing because it took place here in Yaounde."

"Please tell it. What happened?"

22

"Here it is. As you see, I took seriously your suggestion of writing something for the celebration of your daughter's surgical operation as you said that it was the result of God's intervention in your family's life. Why don't you just read it? It is entitled: *A Testimony of Mistaken Identity and God's Timely Intervention*".

Here is the text that I then read silently.

It is often said that people are created in pairs. That is why one could find two persons of no blood relationship having a remarkable resemblance both in physic and manners. More often than not, the issue of mistaken identity occurs at social gatherings, on the streets and even in formal settings where people call out on others by other names but soon realize that they have mistaken their identities. I once suffered the fate of a lady whom I was said to have a remarkable resemblance with. I was not only said to resemble this lady who resided in Douala, but coincidentally, we were said to bear the same name "Maguy". I was victimized, ridiculed, and put to public shame for an act I didn't carry out just because of mistaken identity, where, if not of an angel who vindicated me, the consequences would have been far reaching.

It all happened like this: one evening, twelve years ago, a very close friend of mine came from Douala for a funeral ceremony in Yaounde where I live. She paid me a visit in my home in Biyem-Assi and asked me to accompany her to Nsimeyong where the ceremony was taking place. As soon as we hailed a taxi, she spotted a Littoral matriculated Toyota Tercel car on the other side of the street and told me it belonged to her friends with whom she had traveled from

Douala. She immediately shouted out to them and we crossed over to meet them. The man was in the car alone as his wife had just crossed the street to get something from a shop. We then stood chatting and waiting for her to come back so that we could greet her too. Little did I know that danger awaited me!

This lady had spotted me right from the shop and took me for her rival, a lady she had suspected of having an affair with her husband. To my greatest dismay, this lady I had never seen before dashed out of the shop and headed towards me with a lot of fury in her eyes. She shouted out to me: "Maguy" I was frightened by the fact that she knew my name but I managed to answer "oui". This was too true to be coincidental!

She pounced on me and hooked her fingers in the rasters I was having on my hair and shouted "Donc c'est toi! Voleuse de maris! Donc tu as suivi mon mari jusqu'a Yaoundé? Maintenant tu es morte." [So, it is you! Thief of husbands! You thus followed my husband until Yaounde? Now, you are a dead woman.]

My friend and I were scandalized beyond measure. We both stared at each other speechless because we didn't understand what was going on. What was most disturbing was the fact that she kept shouting: "maman oh! Venez voir alors ce que je te disais!" [Mom, come and see what I have been telling you!] I immediately concluded that this lady was mentally ill and the only solution was to escape her attacks. I tried to release her fingers from my hair but she rooted out some of the "rasters" causing a lot of pain in my head. This struggle attracted a large crowd which started jeering at me. To my greatest surprise, her husband I was hoping could

24

rescue me drove off with speed; because he didn't want to identify himself with a mentally deranged wife.

I was then left to depend on my helpless friend who tried to explain to the crowd that it was a mere resemblance to no avail. Provokingly, this lady pulled out a picture from her hand bag and showed to the crowd. "Ce n'est pas elle ici?" I almost fainted when I saw that the lady in the picture looked exactly like me in color size and facial features. The crowd concluded from the picture that I was no other than the "voleuse de maris," i.e., "thief of husbands." So they rounded me up and the jeers increased.

I felt extremely humiliated, and my friend on her part could go no further to defend me because she had been rendered powerless in the hands of the crowd. Tears ran down my cheeks and I said to myself:- "Poor me! All alone in a strange crowd! What if my husband sees me here? What will he say about me?" I looked around but there was no one to rescue me from the yoke of my enemies. I then lifted up my eyes to where my help could come from (Psalms 121 verse 1 to 2) and said:

"God, if ever I had known this man before, or had an affair with him, let this crowd stampede me. But if you find me innocent, vindicate me so that the truth shall prevail and your name be glorified"

As I lowered my eyes from this prayer, as if I was dreaming, I saw one huge young man break through the crowd and approach me with a lot of vigor. I immediately concluded that it was the end of me. But at last! A miracle was about to happen. God had sent a friend in need, who was no other than one of my students of the Premier class in

Lycée de Mendong where I had been teaching for over five years. He held my hand and shouted out to the crowd:

"Laissez mon prof. d'anglais en paix. Depuis quand est ce qu'elle est devenue voleuse de maris à Douala? Puisque je la connais depuis cinq ans au lycée de Mendong et je n'ai jamais entendu qu'elle vit à Douala. Les malhonnêtes, vous allez payer cher"

[Leave my English teacher in peace. Since when is she a thief of husbands in Duala? I have known her for 5 five years at Mendong High School and I have never heard that she ever lived in Duala. You dishonest people, you will have to pay a high price for this ill-treatment.]

He took over command of the crowd and immediately pulled me across the street like a child and stopped the first taxi that approached. I dropped into it like a dead object and got home pretty late.

I sobbed all night when I recalled the experience but thanked God for rescuing me. My friend had no choice but to follow me home. She equally spent a disturbing night blaming herself all along for dragging me into public disgrace. As for the man, he called me the following morning apologizing for his wife's misconduct. For the lady, I never again saw her or heard of her. The only news I got from my friend again was that from that day on, the couple lived in separation and today, they are divorced. For the Premier student who saved my life, I did every thing possible to find him in school for some compensation but surprisingly I never got any trace of him until I left that institution.

To conclude, remarkable resemblance can bring untold consequences to those who fall victim. I know of cases of twins who have manipulated their twin brother's or twin sister's spouses. I have also heard of cases of people being called ghosts because they resemble people who have died. My own story is just one of those. However it must be admitted that there are equally positive circumstances of mistaken identity in life e.g., helping somebody who resembles another like giving a lift, offering a job or accommodation.

While I was reading it, Margaret kept looking at me. She probably wanted to find out what I thought of it. As she noticed that I was done with the reading, she told me:

"But again, don't you see that this was a real miracle?"

"Margaret, I really do not know what to tell you. I am surely sympathetic with you. I hope that, if we publish your story, there are people who will relate to it and find that, in difficult times, God may answer their prayers when they call upon him. This story of resembling other people has served you in the wrong way. In my case, I remember, when I was at the teacher training college of Bukavu, DRC, there was a lady who supposedly resembled me. At times, I would meet people who asked me if she was my sister. We happened to belong to the same ethnic group. Other people used to say that she resembled my wife. Curiously enough, some people used to tell me that I also resemble my own wife. That lady became our best friend. To tell the truth, I admired her. I found her very beautiful. In fact she always reminded me of a lady that I met in Belgium while I was still very young and that I also admired very much. Her name was Arlette. My eldest daughter got the name of Arlette because of that lady. For this lady who resembled me, I just keep good souvenirs about her. She used to send her daughter to stay with our family because she felt part of our family."

"Sir, you always have interesting stories. When I am with you, I always forget that I am with my teacher. By the way, can you tell me whether your telephone subscription is with Orange or with MTN?"

"It is with Orange. Why?"

"I know why I am asking you. You will find out some day. I have to go. See you."

Two days later, Margaret came back to my office and handed me an Orange card worth 5000 CFA Francs. She told me that she knows that, in times of bereavement, one spends a lot of money on calls. This was her way to contribute to the expenses Georgina's death has caused to my family. I said to myself that Margaret just has a golden heart. I would not say it for many Cameroonians.

To come back to the end of Margaret's story, as soon as she was out, another student came to knock at the door of my office. It was Francine.

"Good morning sir. I have been waiting outside to see you. You took so much time with Margaret. Why?"

"Well, she came to express her condolences," I answered.

"She is not the only person to express them. I too am coming for the same purpose."

I cannot say that I was used to Francine. I never showed her that I liked her. But ladies always know when someone likes them or not. In her case, I am sure she knew that I liked her. Three days earlier, I had asked her what she planned to write her MA thesis on. She told me that she did not know. She then revealed to me that there were other teachers who wanted her to do syntax. I then told her that I really wish her to do what she really likes. She should not feel pressured. I also told her that I also wanted her to take my phonology courses, but that she does not have to specialize in phonology if she does not feel like it.

I guess she must have interpreted that I am interested in her. The truth is that I was highly interested in her. I liked her. I kind of considered her as my daughter and I wanted to be able to protect her, to guide her, to act as a parent for her. I found her very beautiful. She was still young, but I always imagined that one year from now, she would be a full-bloomed woman. She would be one of the most beautiful girls in Cameroon. At the same time, her behavior was so simple. I do not think that she was aware of her beauty. In fact, as we started talking, she told me that she also came because of what I had told her about my daughter. She said that she felt very saddened. At the same time, she said that she had a story that she had written and she wanted me to read it. Hopefully, she hoped that I would publish it, and that it would help convince people that God does intervene in our lives. Her story is so interesting that I will try to recount it just as she gave it to me. She wrote it in French. So, this is my translation.

Could one ever remain insensitive towards the manifestation of God's power? How can one persist in not believing after experiencing the power of the Almighty God?

My name is D.M. Francine, and I am a student in LGT4. I thank my God who, through my sociolinguistics professor, gives me the privilege of making the world know what he has done to me.

Before I start telling my testimony, I would like to remind my readers that I was led to the Lord very early in my life. I did Sunday school which, in my case, has been a decisive step in my way to the Lord. During my adolescence, I got baptized in 2001. Now that you know something of my past, I will tell you how the Lord God demonstrated through me his supremacy and his lordship.

Every normal girl gets menstruations at her puberty. When I reached that age, I was no exception to this natural law. However, what was peculiar in my situation is that, every month, at the beginning of my menses, I felt excruciating pains all day long. It was so painful. I used to lock myself up inside my room, and then, I would sleep on the floor and cry all day long. You imagine how this rendered my parents extremely worried! They did everything to try to find me the right treatment. They thus brought me to different hospitals. Despite the high cost of drugs and their quantity I never got the right cure. To attenuate the pain, I used to take antibiotic drugs a week before the beginning of my menstruations. It seemed to work for a while. But in the end, this treatment was no longer efficient. Every month, I had to spend a whole day in "hell". What rendered it even more painful to me is that I was not sexually active. I then wondered what I might have done to deserve this punishment. I told myself that, if begetting a child was more painful than this, then surely I would die on the operation table before delivering my baby.

One day, as I was listening to the radio, I tuned into a talk show in which the presenter was giving sanitation counsels.

She announced that a herbalist declared that he is able to cure painful menses. I told my parents who did not hesitate to take me to that herbalist. After taking his potions, I did not see any improvement in my condition. On the contrary, it even became worse!

I suffered for five years. One day, I told one of my cousins about this Calvary of mine. That was an opportunity for her to also recount me her own testimony. She said that, until the age of 21, she used to pee in bed. That situation was a consequence of something that occurred to her mother when she carried her pregnancy. The traditional doctor had put a cross on her womb while making incantations. As a consequence, she constantly peed in her bed without realizing it. The day that people in her church prayed for her, she got delivered. Because of this testimony, I turned toward my God to implore his mercy and cure. This cousin of mine then brought me to a friend of my daddy, who was an elder in the church, and whose task is to pray for the sick. After a short interview with him, I took an appointment with him for the following week. During that week, I began to fast everyday from 6 a.m. to 6 p.m. The last day, we met and he prayed for me and I instantly recovered.

I have been fine for three years now. I no longer feel any pain whatsoever. I have been delivered from that illness. From that experience, this is what I have retained: God's power manifests to the broken hearts, to the hearts which are genuinely sincere. The Lord is all powerful and he manifests his almightiness to those who believe in him. Today, I can enjoy life and I sincerely appreciate life because I have been delivered. I give thanks to the Lord. I bless him and praise him with all my hearts. Thank you Lord.

Well, this is a powerful testimony. Imagine all this pain that Francine went through in the past. It does not matter whether it was a pastor or a priest who prayed for her. What is sure, it was someone who really believed in God. Francine also sincerely believed in God and her prayers were heeded. I hope this remains a lesson for us. We should never despair. God does see our suffering. He just wants us to come to him, and He will then deliver us. Praise to God. Amen.

A few days after this, I again met Margaret in my office. She told me that she had been working on her second testimony and that it was almost ready. She simply needed to rewrite it properly. This time, she was not alone. She said that the lady who was with her was her own mother. She told me that she now had better recollections for the events that took place in her testimony because she had been able to ask her mother to explain some cultural details. As I talked to her mother, I had the feeling that she wanted to see me, that is, the person who was going to publish her daughter's testimony because it remains something sacred in her heart. Here is the text of Margaret's second testimony that she gave me a few days later.

I was twelve years old when my two elder brothers and one younger one and I went to our farm some three kilometers from our home. Our mother had traveled, leaving us in our father's care. Before we left for the farm, our father somehow had a premonition and wouldn't let us go. But my elder brothers insisted that our mother had assigned us to weed the whole farm before she returned from her trip.

When we arrived at the farm, we kept our basket of food and clothes under one big tree that had a shade. We then went straight to work, sharing the beds according to ages. At about 2PM, we went and sat under the tree to take our lunch.

Soon, it started drizzling, and we agreed to wait for the rain to stop before we continued the weeding. As we sat under the tree, I heard thunder bolts and I saw lightning that flashed across the sky. Then we went into a deep slumber, all four of us, and slept till 6PM when, suddenly, I woke up from the slumber. I didn't know where I was. I felt a hot pain on my chest like fire burn. Then I struggled to get up and, surprisingly, I realized that my brothers were all lying in awkward positions. It was then that I realized we were still under the tree in the farm. I tried to shake them one after the other, asking them to get up so that we should go home since it was getting dark. My desperate effort continued for about 30 minutes but none of my three brothers woke up. I got angry because I thought they were despising me and I told them "If you don't want to get up, I will go and leave you here."

That said, I left them and started staggering down the hill in the closing darkness. The pain on my chest grew worse. I felt a lot of heaviness on my chest and when I felt it with my fingers, I realized that there were swellings on it. I kept turning back to look if my brothers were following, but I saw none of them. As it had drizzled for long, the foot path down the hill was so slippery and dark. I staggered on like somebody half-drunk. My way was lit by lightning time and again until I reached the motorable road (i.e. the unpaved road in Cameroonian English).

I was in a trance, half awake and half asleep, but I found myself progressing in my journey home. After much effort of trekking, I came to some homesteads about 2 kms away from our home, when I thought of going there to report what had happened to us in the farm, but a question flashed through my mind: 'what am I going to tell them? That my brothers are sleeping in the farm and have refused to get up? No, let me better go and tell my father so that he can go and wake them up." Then I passed by those homesteads and continued.

I thought of the fastest way to arrive home since the motorable road was long and winding. Now another thought came to my mind. "Why don't you take a shortcut that will lead you home faster?" I went down a slope behind the homesteads and reached a small stream below which I thought I would just cross to the other side but, unfortunately for me, the stream had overflowed its banks, hiding all the stones that people stepped on when crossing. I gazed at the stream in the dark in my complete trance and something mysterious happened to me. I suddenly found myself across the stream without making conscious effort to cross it.

I couldn't imagine so to confirm my surprise. I felt my feet with my hands and found that they were not wetted by water. I just continued up another slope to meet the main road with one more kilometer to walk home.

Meanwhile, my father who had waited for us too long called out some men to accompany him to the farm. They took only the main road because they were afraid to cross an over flooded stream, so we bypassed. When I finally got home, I struggled in the dark to find a match and light a local lamp called "trucan." When my aunt who lived just across the road saw the flickering light of the lamp, she immediately came to see who was there. She found me and asked where my brothers were. I recounted the whole tragedy to her with childlike precision.

She immediately understood what had happened and started inspecting my body. When she felt some bumps on my chest, she asked me what they were. As I was almost passing out, I told her in my trance that the lamp had burnt me. She screamed and carried me to her place where she gave me a hot bath and laid me in bed. I heard wailing and rushing footsteps from a distance and they soon died down. I fainted. All that happened thereafter was told to me one month later after I regained consciousness.

When I opened my eyes, the first question I asked was:

"Where are my brothers?"
"Did they get up from the sleep?"
Another aunt who volunteered to stay with us in the hospital just simply pointed at my younger brother on the bed opposite mine. Then I asked him.

"Why did you not remain in the farm?"

Then I kept insisting:

"Where are my two elder brothers?

She said "they are at home," but I realized that all was not well because she started sobbing.

"Why are they not here too?" I continued.
"They would come one day," she replied.

So I was so anxious to see them. We still had to stay in the hospital for two weeks because my wounds had grown septic.

The day we were discharged was a memorable one. People crowded the roadsides to see us pass in a van and some even followed us right to our house. I had never seen a sympathetic crowd like that before. When we arrived home, all that was on my mind was to see my two elder brothers. I went straight into the house but no glimpse of them. Instead, I noticed that furniture arrangement in the sitting room was upset and things looked like there had been a ceremony in our house. I also noticed that my mother had grown so frail and my father so sorrow-stricken. I was confused. So I got up in the evening and went behind our house. To my greatest dismay, I saw two mounts of freshly dug up earth. As I was trying to make out what could have been planted there, one of my playmates came towards me and asked:

"Did you see the lightning puppy that stroke you four in the farm and two of your brothers died?"

"What do you mean by lightning puppy?" I asked her.

"They said that the lightning sent to kill somebody goes like a small dog and perches on a tree before exploding into fire," she said.

"I didn't see any puppy," I answered calmly.

"Then it means that you were not vigilant enough to see it," she continued while laughing.

I reflected backwards to the scene but I did not remember how it all happened. Then my mind went back to the two freshly dug-up mounts of earth and I asked her:

"What then is planted here?"

"Your two big brothers of course!" she exclaimed.

"So as they were sleeping like that in the farm they didn't get up," I asked desperately.

"They slept like that and then died," she said casually.

"So if I dig this place, will I see them?" I continued in desperation.

"Yes, the first one was buried there and the second one here," she said pointing to the graves at intervals.

It was then that the truth dawned on me and I burst into tears. But, surprisingly, instead of consoling me, my friend asked:

"Why are you crying? You should instead be happy that you have escaped their menaces."

I felt instantly relieved when I thought of how those elder brothers used to beat me whenever I disobeyed them. But again, I would have preferred the beatings than losing them entirely.

My friend was the only source I ever got the true story from.

Now, how can this mysterious phenomenon be understood or interpreted? Scientifically, it is said to be a flash of bright light in the sky produced by electricity moving between clouds or from clouds to the ground, especially attracted by iron deposits. Trees too are a good conductor of lightning. Hence, this is what could be considered a scientific interpretation of our predicament.

But in the North West Region of Cameroon, traditional belief has it that lightning can be sent to warn or kill a debtor or an enemy. My father's misfortune came as a result of a piece of land he bought from a wicked and jealous family. I stand as an exhibit of such circumstances, and I still have indelible scars left on my belly. (By the way, as I told this story to my sociolinguistics teacher, i.e., Prof. Mutaka the editor of this book, he insisted that I show him those scars. I did. A personal note from Mutaka: I wish to tell the reader that I confirm it. It was not that I did not trust Margaret Chenemo Neh, but I wanted to make sure that people who would read the story believe her when they know that I have seen that scar with my own eyes.) To me, this is unquestionable because, on that same fateful day, lightning struck three of our farms in search of us. In every farm, a tree was burnt up. But some incidents are said to be natural.

In the case of man initiated lightning, it is said that the act is carried out by some specialists who could also hold back rain from falling. Man made lightning is set up by a mixture of gun powder and certain herbs and then the composed mixture is blown into the air during a downpour while chanting the names of the persons to be destroyed. The lightning is to go everywhere in search of the victims. When the lightning leaves the sender, it goes like a small fire bird or a small fire puppy and perches on a tree, then splits into stripes of fire and electrocutes the victim. After its mission has been accomplished, it signals in the sender's medicine pot and he jubilates.

The "lightning doctors" render services to clients who come and pay them to eliminate or warn their debtor or enemies. When it is just to warn the victim, the amount is less but when it is to destroy, the amount is huge. The fees also vary with respect to the number of people involved. In my case, four of us were destined to die but God's saving power spared two of us.

I wonder if these lightning specialists could not work positively for the good of the community by generating electricity to light the villages rather than destroy souls.

Nevertheless, this awful tragedy that has never parted company with me since I was twelve has impacted tremendously on my life, transforming misfortune into inner strength. As I grew up I was determined to change my family's mourning into bliss and God has always been on my side. I moved from glory to glory in several fields of endeavor and that was a befitting recompense for the death of my two elder brothers. I furthered my education, got married and had four kids, naming the first two boys after my late brothers. My husband was so good to me that he inspired me to gain entry into the Advanced College Education and subsequently into the Public Service where I now earn a reasonable salary. This enabled me to sponsor my siblings through their education and also to support my parents who were fast ageing. Before my father died, he usually made a consolatory statement to himself. "One girl equals five boys." And on his sick-bed, he said his successor was to be the girl who changed his old tune to a new one. This was in line with the song by Abba:

"I crossed the stream; I have a dream to help me cope in everything.
You can see the wonder of a fairy tale
You can tell the future even if it fails
I believe in Angel, something good in everything I see
I believe in Angel, when the time is ripe
I crossed the stream,
I have a dream."

As I finished reading this written testimony, I sighed.

"Yes, your story is really amazing. We must publish it. I simply do not know what to say about it. I am sorry that you lost your brothers. But that is the way life is. I am not sure though if it is the kind of story that people will believe and that can change their lives."

"Well, at least I know that I am telling you the truth. If someone does not want to see the hand of God in this miracle, there is nothing that I can force on him. Even until now, I have never understood how I was able to cross the river when getting back from the farm. In my mind, this is an unquestionable testimony that God does intervene in our daily lives," she concluded and then bid me goodbye.

As I left my office, I met Marietou in the hall. She looked worried. She did not see me at first. So I greeted her. Now because she is Muslim, I need to make a sort of flashback during the wake-keeping at my place. A long discussion occurred, a discussion that is likely to help us understand our Muslim compatriots.

Chapter 4

A Muslim Woman's deep trust in God

As soon as Astou heard about Georgina's death, she called me. I was extremely embarrassed because I had not had time to call neither her nor her husband about the bad news. This time, I was alone because my wife was still in Ghana with the corpse.

Khadija, that is, Astou's daughter, had been Georgina's very first friend on this planet Earth. She was about 2 years old. Her family lived just above us in a building that the university rented for the foreigners. For my own family, it was the first time that we really got into close contact with a Muslim family. Astou's husband, Mamadou Sow, is a medical doctor. I must say that I found him very pious. He was a faithful churchgoer, more precisely, someone who strictly observed the precepts of the Koran. He was actually the only urologist in Cameroon and because of that, many political authorities knew him. He was certainly close to the Muslim political authorities, particularly those from the Northern provinces of Cameroon.

When Georgina was about three years old, she developed an infection on her chest. We did not know what caused it. We thought that it might be related to her state. We naturally showed that infection to Dr. Sow. His immediate reaction was:

"Bring her to the hospital tomorrow. I will need to operate on her."

I hope you understand which kind of person he was. He was ready to help. And in his case, it was not for money. In fact, during our stay here in Cameroon, he is the only surgeon who ever operated Georgina free of charge. The other operation that Georgina underwent was at Etoug-ebe. We observed that, because of her condition, the flesh on one side of the neck was not correct. The doctors decided to operate on her. For that operation, we had to pay for everything. It is as if the hospital had nothing and that we just had to give money for anything that would be used during the operation. In addition, we had to pay a caution of at least 150,000 francs for an operation that seemed so benign. I am not writing this to complain about the conditions found in the local hospitals. I just want to mention it to emphasize the fact that Dr. Sow, a Muslim urologist, proved to us that Muslims can have the best of hearts in helping the neighbor. Isn't this that our pastors in the Christian religion always encourage us to do?

To come back to the wake keeping, a number of people had congregated at my place. At a certain time, we saw Professor Sow and his entire family enter our house. This was amazing. Usually when people came, either the husband would come, or the wife, or the husband and wife, but not an entire family. It was understandable that the entire Sow family would come because they had been our first neighbors in Cameroon. In a sense, Georgina had been their daughter as well.

It is an African custom that, during wake-keeping, people speak about anything. It is probably meant to prevent an atmosphere of sadness in the house. It is true that, when the bereaved is there, certain women start wailing as soon as they enter the house. This is not what happened on that day. It did happen when my wife came back from Ghana. On that particular evening, what was interesting is a discussion that ensued among the wake-keepers about religion.

One of the participants is a faithful Christian. His nickname is Cardinal. The reason he was called Cardinal is because he had studied the Christian doctrine in order to understand it better. For his secondary school, he had been at a seminary and he was quite knowledgeable in theological issues about the Christian religion. He seemed to also know about the Muslim religion. Dr. Sow, as I said, is a faithful Muslim. He too seemed very knowledgeable in the Muslim religion. The discussion that ensued thus put two people who belonged to the two main religions found in the African continent.

I cannot recall all the details of the discussion, but what I retained from what Professor Sow said about the Christian religion is that, both Muslims and Christians accept the ancient testament. Where they differ is that the Muslims accept Jesus as a prophet and not as the son of God. One question that kept recurring was whether the God of the Muslims is the same God of Christians. For Dr. Sow, this was not even an issue because God cannot change. He is the same God. During the discussion, we realized that, throughout history, Muslims and Christians have been warring in the name of God. Lots of people have died in these wars. The war of the crusades that lasted 100 years is one such example where it is not clear who was right and who was wrong.

As I saw Marietou, I recalled that discussion. In my mind, I hoped that Marietou would give me an answer as I had asked her, and the other Muslims in class, to help us understand that their God is also our God and that God does intervene in their lives. If we could obtain testimonies that

God has heard individual prayers, then we will know that this must be the same God.

Marietou told me she had prepared her testimony in writing. I was pleased and hoped to find answers to some of my questions. In the following paragraphs, I will give it to you. I simply want to tell you that it was fascinating. But it never answered the specific question whether God answered the prayers of the Muslims in the same way as He answers Christians' prayers. In fact, the impression that I personally got is that God cannot be said to belong to a given religion. He is God. What he requires from us is that we be faithful to him. Our religions always have something that reveals what God is. But they will not encompass what he really is. In getting true testimonies about God's intervention in our lives, we can continue nurturing the divine bud that is in al of us, Christians, Muslims, Jewish, Buddhists, etc. This divine bud is true and it lives in the hearts of every individual. It is beyond religion. Our religious leaders might be fighting, or misleading us on certain theological issues, but when we know that God is with us, He will talk to us and operate miracles in us.

Let me translate again what Marietou had to say about God's intervention in her life as a Muslim.

To begin with, what I will tell you might look simplistic because many people among you certainly live such experiences in their daily lives. The peculiarity in my story lies in the way we interpret these daily events, the effects that they can operate in the life of an individual as has been my case.

In order to understand all this, I have to tell you something about my past life. In fact, the testimonies that will follow are from my personal life. I have been and still remain a Muslim woman since my birth. And like every believer, I was raised in the strict respect of the religious values. When I say "religious," without precision, it is because I have never lived in a milieu that is exclusively Islamic. I have spent my life surrounded by people of different religious confessions. All my friends did not share necessarily my religious beliefs. Moreover, I went to a Catholic school. I have put ash on my face on ash day like the Catholics during their fasting period. I have attended masses, sung religious Christian canticles, and very often, I have participated in the Christmas celebration. In fact I have grown without ever worrying whether I was different from other people. To me, they were Christians and they went to a Christian church, and as a Muslim, I went to a mosque. Was there a Christian God and a Muslim God? I know nothing about that. I simply knew that I had deep faith: faith in an all powerful God, faith in a unique God. In this paper, I will certainly have recourse to certain aspects of my religion but it will not certainly be about a Muslim God or a Christian God. It is on the basis of this faith that I have built my childhood, my adolescence, and now my adult life. I have always believed in the power and almightiness of the Lord God without the slightest doubt. I have felt his presence in every cell of my body, on the street, in a taxi, in a room where I was locked up all alone, in the presence of people or alone. To me, God has always intervened in every instant of my life.

Nothing of all that I will tell you is superstition or dogma. As I told you, it is a sensation that I feel since my childhood: the constant presence of God in my life. The link between God and me is like the link that exists between a master and his slave, a husband and his wife, a father and his daughter, a boyfriend and his girlfriend. God naturally participates to all the events of my life and I always invite him to do it. He is present in my moments of joy and sadness, and I never miss an opportunity to praise him or to thank him. When I have a problem, doubts, or worries, I confide myself to him and ask him to advise me. And believe me, he always responds. How does he do it? He does it through a sin, an image, an event in my life or the life of another person that I have to be able to interpret.

I still remember this event, when I was still in my teens. More precisely, I was about 14 years old. As is a habit in my family, the anniversary is highly important. It is a great moment of communion, joy and new resolutions for the person who celebrates his anniversary by adding one more year. One week and a half before my fourteenth anniversary, I became suddenly sick. I was so sick that, for the first time in my life, I had to spend the night in the hospital. To tell the truth, I have always been considered as the strongest of my family. I was almost never sick. And if I happened to feel sick, I never stayed in bed more than a single day. That day, I really fell badly and the medical doctors could not detect what I was suffering from. After a few days, my parents decided to bring me back home. At home, my mother was constantly at my side as if she was afraid that if she were to get away from me, something was going to happen. The house was so quiet and sad and I could read this sadness in the eyes of my parents and brothers and sisters that I realized that I had affected them so much. Then, from my bed, I started calling on God to help me. I prayed that I did not want that the celebration of an anniversary to become associated to a great loss and deep sadness. Much more importantly, I prayed that he removes all this sadness from their eyes as it was making me suffer even more. My mother was holding a scapular in one hand and the other was always on my side. I know that she too prays hard. She had one hand on my head. Although her prayer was silent, I could feel the depth of her faith in

God as she was imploring Him through the pressure of this hand on my face. And to this scenario, add the one from my father who no longer left his rug of prayer. Did you know that God always heeds our prayers? He may not react when you want him to, but he always reacts at the appropriate time according to his will. Two days before my fourteenth anniversary, I rose from my bed without staggering, that is, just as I used to do it every morning. No more deep feelings of uneasiness, no more violent headaches, no more dizziness and no more weak legs. Everything just got back to normal as if by a magic wand. On the d-day, it was our small nuclear family that was so happy when they woke up to wish me a happy anniversary as if the episode of my sudden sickness never happened.

You know, there are at times things that happen to us and that render us sad, that make us suffer that one feels like detesting the world and its creator. But, as I have said, only God knows when it is the right time. He makes us suffer in order to reveal the good thing in us or from suffering he reveals us sometime later its positive side.

I have never been the assiduous pupil or the best in a class. However, I have always made efforts to succeed in what I do and mostly for not being the last. Oh yes. I have known failures in my school life just like many other pupils I guess. And every failure always meant more efforts, more work. I must acknowledge that, up till a certain age, I did not harbor any real ambitions. My sisters had always been the best in everything that they did and my sluggishness constituted a real problem for my parents. To remedy this sluggishness, my father decided to let me spend my vacations with my elder sister on a university campus. I behaved as if I was going to become a freshman in the university. I must admit that my first contact with the student world produced a real positive trigger on me. It certainly enabled me to succeed at my exam and then I decided to take hold of my life and fixed goals I was to reach. I was so enthusiastic by my resolutions that I did not allow them to be hampered by anything. I felt I had become big enough that I had to decide for myself without any intervention of anybody else. In fact, I did not stand any contradiction to my choices. However, when one is still living with her parents and that one is still in her puberty, it is very difficult not to allow them to intervene in your life. One evening, as I had opposed a prohibition that my father imposed on me, the worst happened. With my daddy, the bone of contention was so violent and the words were so harsh that I felt so disrupted. As I was so angry, I screamed at him telling him that I detested him so much and that I detested everybody else because no one dared intervene in my favor. It was in that context that I started the last straight line for my final exam. Two days after this argument with my family, I was to take the sports exam for my GCE level (in French, the Baccalauréat). Unfortunately, I was still disturbed emotionally. I was unable to run my life and decide which was which. My state made me so sour that I was angry at my own family. That evening, I started feeling bad, but I thought I did not have to worry about it. Unfortunately, it is a week that I will spend lying very miserable in my bed. The reason is that, since that quarrel, I stopped eating and did not socialize with other people. Moreover, I did not want to make them the pleasure to show them how weak I was because of my pride. All the initiatives of my mother and my younger sisters and brothers to know what was wrong with me were vain. It was within that context that I took the final written exam of my GCE.

To better understand all this, I must mention an important aspect. My parents have always endeavored to protect us and they always intervene in what we do. Although we are not that extroverted, it is a sacred custom in my family to always wish good luck and to encourage the other in everything that they do. That morning when I had to take my GCE exam, I left my home with the usual words "I am leaving." Not even a single look from my parents or my sisters. Nobody wished me good luck and "have a good day." I became so sad that it was with eyes full of tears that I arrived at the center where I had to take that exam. All this sadness showed up all day long on the day of my final exam. When the results came, they were obviously not good at all. If I say, "obviously," it is because I knew that there was something missing. You will certainly react 'even people who are cursed succeed at their exams." I must say that everybody does not have the same destiny. My family is just part of my destiny. While I was angry, I had decided that after obtaining my secondary school diploma, I would go and live somewhere else, far from those who did not really understand me or did not apparently like me. If I had succeeded at my exam that year, I believe that a deep gap would have been created between me and my family. I am not superstitious, believe me. I am just convinced that everything that we do has to bear the blessings of our parents. My parents had always wished me good luck and given the right counsels before all of my exams. Then, why could I have thought that I could live a normal life without their blessing? If God had answered my prayer of letting me succeed, I would have lived probably separated from my parents. My failure turned out to be a positive thing in that it pushed me to get closer to my family. My youngest sister is the one who comforted me all day long. My twin brothers who are always very noisy respected my sadness and my silence. As for my father, when I called him, he simply said: "do not worry. This was the first time that you were trying to take this exam. I can see that you will succeed next year." It is then that all the tears that I had kept in my chest flew. God did not answer my wish of succeeding to my GCE exam and then to leave my family, a wish that would have caused me more problems. He had in fact answered it in a different way: the one that my pride did not want me to accept. Again, God had heeded the good side of my profound sadness and he had intervened once more in my life.

The following testimony that also concerns my personal life is as painful as the preceding one. Some years ago, I met a young man. I cannot say that he really fulfilled the conditions that I require in an ideal future husband, but he looked a true believer and he respected me a great deal. That is the way I saw him. Despite my resolution I took as soon as I settled in town, notably, that my priorities would be my studies and nothing else, I decided to respond positively to what I perceived as his love feelings towards me. Everything went on very well: lots of laughing when we were together, and a kind of complicity developed between us. I was happy. I started raising questions in my mind. I was somehow worried about his changing behavior. It is true that we never made any promise to each other but I had always been frank with him and therefore I found it unacceptable that he would hide certain things to me. The worst thing is that I began suspecting that he had a relationship with a girl who was very close to me, someone I considered as a sister to me because we grew up together and have spent our life almost together. It is true that, in a certain way, we had decided to keep our relation secret for the simple reason that none of us really knew what he really expected from that relationship. One day, everything exploded: he admitted his relationship with my friend and told me how much they loved each other, and her decision to get engaged to him. I guess that, at that time, I should have wished them good luck and go away. Unfortunately, I did not. I could not stand his duplicity: to entertain relations with two close friends without saying anything to any of them. I also have to admit that my pride could not stand that he got rid of me for another girl, whatever that girl could be. All the worst thoughts that one can have ran through my mind. I felt things that I did not think myself able to feel and do against my neighbor: aversion, deep distrust, disappointment, and hatred. I felt hatred towards the world around me and towards them. I was even angry against God as I thought he had abandoned me to suffer. What I now know is that I was taking my pride as betrayed love. I had become a shadow of my own being as I even thought about hurting myself. Then, one evening, this friend of mine came and found me in that state. She told me: "even if people do something wrong to you, never do something wrong to yourself." Suddenly, I realized that I was totally wrong, that I had misjudged the events that were happening in my life. God loves me so much that, instead of abandoning me after I had turned my back to him, he once more came to my help. To ask for his forgiveness, and mostly, to renew my devotion to him, I started fasting for a relatively long period of time. I did it in order to purify myself and remove away from me all the bad thoughts that had started finding roots in me. I decided to be spending my time praying, imploring his forgiveness and asking for his help. I did not want to become a disappointed woman, sour, deeply wounded because of jealousy and mean. I really started praying hard so that he might take all these negative vibrations away from me. I must reveal that God heeded my prayers again. How did I know that he had answered my prayers? Well, I just felt it. At the end of my fasting period, I felt entirely purified, with the sensation that I was born again. I did end my relationship with the young boy but all my dull feelings were gone away from me. Whenever I meet him, I just greet him without any resentment whatsoever. As to his fiancée that I consider as my sister, the link between us has even strengthened. Everything has come back to normal.

The following testimony that is my last one might seem to you abnormal. It is abnormal in that most of you will wonder why I give it as a testimony of God's intervention in my life and how he intervenes in my life. To such a question, I will just answer as I have always answered through the following poem. (I give the original one in French and will give a translation after it).

Les Miracles
Très souvent on les cherche
Prie, implore, hurle pour
Alors que les miracles c'est nous.
Oui, les miracles c'est la vie autour de nous
Les miracles c'est l'air que nous respirons
Les miracles c'est notre corps, nos sensations
Ce sont nos yeux
Qui nous permettent de voir et d'admirer à la juste valeur
Les miracles, c'est notre bouche
Les miracles ce sont nos bras, nos pieds
Les miracles, c'est notre tête

Qui nous permet de juger et d'évaluer de façon
rationnelle
Les miracles, ce sont nos espoirs
Qui nous permettent de voir en demain un autre jour.
Les miracles, ce sont nos peurs
Nos craintes de tomber et ne pouvoir nous relever
Les miracles, ce sont nos ambitions,
Oui, les miracles, c'est nous.
L'espoir, les peurs, la joie, l'ambition, les rêves
Que d'autres ont perdu ou n'ont jamais connu.

The Miracles
Very often people look for them
 Pray, implore, howl
Although we are the miracles
Yes, the miracles, it is life around us
The miracles, it is the air that we breathe
The miracles, it is our body, our sensations
It is our eyes
Which enable us to see and admire to its right value
The miracles, it is our mouth
The miracles, they are our arms, our feet
The miracles, it is our head
Which enables us to judge and evaluate in a rational way
The miracles, it is our hopes
Which enable us to see through tomorrow another day
The miracles, it is our fears
Our fears from falling and no longer getting up
The miracles, it is our ambitions
Yes, the miracles, we are the miracles
The hope, the fears, the joy, the ambition, the dreams
That other people have lost or have never known.

53

The gist of this poem is simply to say that God's intervention is like a miracle. These are miracles in our lives and of our lives. Every miracle in our life is God's intervention. We do not have to always look for miracles through astounding realizations of our lives because the mere element, the mere event or image that is the smallest and which may be considered as insignificant is a whole miracle. Do you think that you are really protected against becoming crazy one day because you do not have any germs that could make you become crazy in your life? Do you think your future is perfect because you succeed in every endeavor of yours? Do you think you will have normal children because you are normal and that it is the other who is condemned to have such abnormal children because he was born with a germ of handicap? In that case, how do you then explain that I am beautiful and my child is ugly? That I am smart but my brother is less brilliant. That I am weak but the other is strong. Well, the reason is simple: God intervenes in our lives and around us in different ways, that is, in our reactions of feeling them, of appreciating them. For me, every single small event in my life, in my neighborhood, even with people I live with and that I do not know is a means of communication with God. Your reaction might be that I can live while ignoring all this as this is not an issue in life. I say no. I believe that God also gave me the power of listening, of communication, of making sense of events, of observing. Therefore, the fact of seeing through other people's joy to create my own joys is a perfect example of God's intervention. The fact of seeing other people crying make me realize how lucky I am, just as my tears stop flowing when I see other people happy. Other people's suffering reveals my chance and mostly they make me realize that I should never forget the existence of the other human beings.

Most probably, as you read these testimonies, your reaction will be "you live an unrealistic life." I do not think so. I have always said that there is no ideal situation in life. We are the ones to align our desires, our wishes with reality. The reality is that God is everywhere with us and in us. We may not pay attention to this fact, as is probably the case of your own loved ones. But God somehow always intervenes in our lives even through what makes you suffer profoundly.

As I finished reading these testimonies, I started wondering whether I am really different from Marietou. I believe I am just like her. Or rather, I would like to be able to behave like her, especially when she says that she completely has her faith in God. There certainly must be a divine bud that is in all of us and that manifests itself through innocent people, whatever their religion is. When you take the whole life of Georgina, you can consider her as a divine bud. She went back to God while she was still unsullied by the various evils we often confront in this world.

Chapter 5

When A Muslim Faces Christ

I believe one of Marietou's testimonies that left a lasting impression on me is her poem. It made me realize that we are the miracles and that everything we participate in can be seen as a miracle. As I was thinking again about Georgina's life, I wondered what lasting impression she could then leave on people. It is true that only the people who had been in contact with her know her. She has never had a life like that of Michael Jackson whose death a few weeks after her death was a world event. Everybody got stuck to the TV because we remembered his songs; we thought about his wealth, we were eager to listen to the obituaries that would be said in his favor. There is even a member of the American Congress who proposed that his name should be inscribed in the annals of the US as a hero who has changed the face of the world. I remember one pastor saying about him that, if the current president of the United States, Barack Obama, was elected, it is also partly because of the way Michael Jackson had prepared the minds of young American people for about forty years to no longer see race as a divide between people. In a sense, he was right. Who could ever think that a black person could be elected president in the most powerful nation of the world?

Again, Georgina's life does not contain any of these extraordinary things. And yet, if she is a saint, and in my mind, she is a saint, and she is certainly looking at me from heaven, what impact could she then leave onto the world?

The answer must be in her simple life. More precisely, in the way she was able to express things through her example.

Let me just tell you how I discovered the other facet of Georgina. First, you need to know that Georgina was the second girl in a family with three children. Her elder sister, Arlette, was ten years older than her. She was much luckier in her life, partly because she spent her early years in the United States. When her parents moved to Cameroon, she made an effort to adapt to Cameroonian life, but she never renounced her American way of living. Although her father was a university teacher, she succeeded to convince him to let her finish her high school at an American school, called "Rain Forest International School" and that was run by SIL (Summer Institute of Linguistics). After her high school, she then went to the Catholic University. She somehow decided that she did not want to obtain her MA diploma in Cameroon because she was a foreigner. She wanted to obtain it in the States. That is how she succeeded to obtain a visa and leave for the States.

Where Georgina comes in is that Arlette left a deep hole in the life of her family. She was used to everything that the new technology brings: the latest models of the telephone, how to play songs on a DVD reader, etc. Curiously enough, everything that Arlette seemed to be the only one to know in the family, Georgina knew it. She was able to make all the gadgets function very well as if Arlette had never left. If something went wrong, she is the one who would always find a solution.

Where Georgina impressed me the most is when her mother left for the DRC. Her grandmother, that is, Jacky's mother, was very sick, and she had called for her daughter. Georgina's family was then left without a mother who always planned everything for it, cooked for it, managed the house, including ensuring a good discipline for the children in the house. Since I have been speaking about a family of three children, at this stage, I should reveal that, after Arlette left for the States, Eric came from the DRC to live with the family. This means that Georgina had her younger sister, Nadine, and her younger brother, Eric. As their father, I must recognize that I have never been the best father. I have always been busy with my academic stuff and have always trusted Jacky, my wife, to run the house. With her absence, it would certainly become very difficult. Before leaving for the DRC, Jacky employed a woman who would be coming to cook for us. This way, we would still continue to live a normal life.

Now, what I have to reveal is that Georgina took up the role of Jacky as our mother. She would be the one to know what we would eat. She was able to look after the children, make sure that they are doing their home works. Under her stewardship, she and Eric always found time to wash our clothes and subsequently iron them. Eric would use the table in the girls' room and Georgina would use the table in the living room for ironing. I knew that she was left-handed but I never imagined that she could tirelessly iron such large piles of clothes with her left hand. She was simply amazing. I had always thought that she was handicapped and that she was this little Georgina who would always remain short because of her congenital scoliosis. The real Georgina was a different one. It was someone who knew to behave like a full-fledged mother.

With her death, I could not prevent thinking about the way one can convey the best message through one's exemplary actions. I am certainly one of those people who feel extremely embarrassed when a so-called born again asks me in public if I have accepted Jesus in my life. Or, when you go to some protestant church services, the pastor asks you to give testimonies of what Jesus has done in your life. What these "religious" people want to hear is that you be able to say that you are "a born again," that you have given completely your life to Jesus.

When I am asked such a question, I feel completely embarrassed. Even if I have given my life to Jesus, why would I start telling it to someone unknown to me? Wouldn't this be a way of boasting? In religious matters, I know that no one can boast to be the perfect example of Jesus' life on earth. To tell the truth, the people who usually boast as "born again" and who proclaim it everywhere in the streets, I tend to consider them as those Pharisees that Jesus reprimanded because they like to show off. Jesus said that their reward is in the pride that they receive from men, not from God. Worse still, if you start scratching beneath the layers of such people who proclaim themselves as "born again," you are bound to discover inconsistencies. Try to examine how they manage their finances. Try to find out how they get their money. Some might be getting donations but, try to see how they get those donations. Try to see how these people behave towards the poor. I have never seen a single person on this earth who would be able to do what Jesus required from his true disciples: sell everything that you have, give it to the poor, and then follow me. How many people are able to do that? This is a sensitive topic. I do not believe that we have to boast in public by saying that we are the perfect examples of Jesus' life on earth. Our true test should rather be in our actions. And that is where we could draw inspiration from Georgina's life. When I say Georgina, I could also refer to any other person you know in your life and who has been proving that he is a real follower of Jesus through his example.

Despite my personal aversion to those "religious" people who boast of being the perfect examples of "born again" Christians, I do admire a great deal those who are able to defend their Christian faith in public. This is a real weakness in me. I am not one of the people who will defend a specific theological doctrine because I am Catholic or Protestant or Muslim for that matter. Again, this has to do with what I perceive as divine bud that can manifest in people of various faiths. I must say that extremists and fanatics literally scare me. It does not matter whether you are a Catholic fanatic, a Protestant fanatic, or a Muslim fanatic. To me, they are not different. I am afraid of any person who believes that it is his only way of perceiving the religious truth that is correct. Such people are always dangerous. As a Catholic, maybe one of the reasons I like our present Pope is that he is human. He knows that we have to be tolerant in our behavior, especially as we deal with other religions. When his talk about the Muslims was misinterpreted, he declared that one has to know when it is the right time to also proclaim the word of God. You will never gain Muslims' sympathy if you start telling them that their religion is totally wrong because it is not mentioned in the Bible. Worse still, you will never succeed to make them repent if you start telling them that they will all go to hell because they have not espoused your Christian brand of religion. The same goes among the different religious sects that flower in the Christian religion.

The reason I mention all this is because, among my sociolinguistics students, there is a girl I nonetheless greatly admire because she was able to defend her Christian faith in front of her classmates. Her name is Kamdem Simo Gaelle Euphrasie.

I should point out that the majority of these students are Bamileke. For people who have lived in Cameroon, they certainly know that Bamileke are very much attached to their traditional customs. One such custom is the cult of the skull. From a strictly Christian point of view, it is not clear why someone should still be revering the dead ancestors, through their skulls, and believe that they are the intermediaries between God and them. But these are beliefs and you cannot change people's mind because you have espoused a western-type of judgment values. As the coordinator of the class, I could distinctly see that most Bamileke are not ready to abandon their skull worshiping. But Gaelle was able to go against what her Bamileke classmates deeply believed in because of her Christian faith. I will not say that she is a fanatic. But what I know, she has a very rich experience, and hopefully, she can move mountains from what she has done. In the following text, I will let you read her response to the question of God's intervention in our lives. The original text is in French. The following is my translation.

She entitled her paper as: *Testimonies of God's miracles in the spiritual milieu*

God is the same yesterday, today and for ever. As we know him today for having saved the dying and dead, there is no sickness or difficulty which would be beyond his power in the life of whoever abandons his life to him with a repenting heart.

In this paper, I will give a testimony in spirit and truth of what the Lord Jesus has done in my life and the life of my brothers. I will then talk about the deliverance of a girl whose name is Georgette, of the empowering of the demon of failures linked to malediction. Thirdly, I will talk about the restoration of a marriage that had been shattered for a long time, and show that this restoration has been the living hand of God. Fourthly, I will talk about a woman's resurrection. I will then talk about a Muslim person who made an authentic encounter with Jesus who made him change his life completely. I will also recount the story of a thug who, after receiving a shot in the stomach, fell into a coma. As he was now abandoned and thought dead in a hospital, he found himself facing a cross soaked in blood, and that was the beginning of his new life full of the love of God and of his Words for the salvation of the lost souls. The very last testimony will recount how God used pastor Tchinde to deliver a young woman who was dying from HIV/AIDS as well as the case of three sisters who succeeded to escape from arson thanks to God's intervention.

To begin with, I have to admit that the Lord God has accomplished great things in my life. I was bisexual, in other words, I used to go out with men but also with women. One day, just on the eve of the year 2007, our housework at my place who was in fact far younger than me in terms of age, was seized by the Spirit of God and she started speaking to us as God's messenger. She was prophesizing by telling us that the Lord asks of us to hope in him, to keep ourselves in his presence and that he would accomplish the desire of our hearts. While talking to us, one had the impression that she was reading what is in our hearts. She was insisting by saying: 'do not doubt, do not doubt." I saw my younger sister, the very last one who was born a few months back, staggering as if she was going to fall down, as she was full with the presence of God. We took hold of her to make her sit down.

When she recovered her senses, she went away from us to the kitchen. The prophecy was still going on, and then I saw my younger sister who immediately followed me, burst into tears. She was not doing any noise; you just had to observe her to realize that she was crying. Suddenly, my sister who had gone away came back and talked to her elder sister who was crying.

"Why do you doubt? Do not doubt any more please!"

I was really astounded by what was happening at home. I then raised my eyes towards the sky and started praying silently, asking the Lord to touch me. I did not get to the end of my prayer when, suddenly, I found myself lying on the floor. I heard the voice of the housewife, near me, who kept on prophesying. Through her, the Lord told me that he was cleansing me from all improprieties and that He was washing my sullen hands. This visit of the Lord instantly changed me completely. I renounced my habit of fornication and my lesbian life. I decided to hate the sin in general in order to love God and his justice. Since then, I can only give testimony of the love and the marvels of God everywhere I go. For me, the work of salvation is the greatest miracle of God as it is the guarantee of eternal life.

However, two years prior to the visitation of the Lord, my mother who had already accepted the Lord was praying hard for our success at school, that is, for my brothers and me. We had no doubt that failure was looming in the horizon as we were about to present our exams. My elder brother who had never failed was doing his BTS for the fourth time; I, as the second child in the family, was presenting the GCE (Baccalauréat) for the third time; my younger sister was presenting her GCE exam for the second time, and our youngest sister was presenting the GCE exam for the first time.

That year, my mother had engaged herself in a spiritual combat. She was resolutely decided, through fasting and prayers, to fight our failure that had been decreed on her children. The Lord operated the miracle. We all succeeded at our exams, except my immediate follower, that is my younger sister who had rebelled in secret against my parents. Fortunately, the Lord had pity on her and, with his bountiful graces, she obtained the GCE diploma the following year, the BTS in hotel business and restoration, two years later. She was even the top student (major in French) of her school year. God really made of her a surprise in the family. From an unexpected grace, the Lord has put me as the top girl on the list of the "Licence en lettres bilingues," during the spring session (that the author called "la session normale").

Since the day I gave my life to Jesus, I feel completely delivered from malaria. As he rightly said in his words, through the wounds of Jesus, I have received his grace of deliverance from any curse. As a matter of fact, I could not spend a whole year without becoming sick, especially with malaria.

The other testimony is that of a woman who was affected by the HIV/AIDS virus and for whom the Lord intervened for her cure at a time when the doctors in the hospitals were unable to treat her to keep her alive. She was only expecting her death when her mother heard that God could make miracles through Pastor Tchinde in a Christian ministry of prayers called MISEM (Ministère International Semence et Moisson). When they brought her there, she was unable to walk by herself; she could not even cling onto someone else to support her, or to sit down. She was completely exhausted and powerless. No muscle in her body was functioning. When she was brought to the location of the prayers, the Christians simply laid her down on the floor where she stayed during all the prayer session. One day, women prayed to the extent that they started crying to God for her. The wife of the pastor who was conducting the prayer lifted part of her dress to show to the assembly to what extent her physical body was damaged and she then said to the assembly:

"Look how she is dying. Look carefully at her body. Imagine that she was your own child"

The assembly became so compassionate as they looked at the skeleton that they started calling loudly the name of God through the name of Jesus. As a consequence, the Lord intervened powerfully. She recovered progressively to the extent that, after doing the HIV test, she was declared completely cured from that disease. Today, she is no longer HIV positive. She has gained weight and she has an average lovely body today. It would be nearly impossible for someone who had never seen her to know and to accept that she was about to die of HIV/AIDS. Since then, she has been walking in the ways of the Lord Jesus.

The Lord also did, through this ministry, something that is unbelievable for people without faith but wholly credible for those who believe in the name of Jesus Christ. Through that Pastor, the Lord has resuscitated a woman who had just died a few days earlier. The pastor looked at the sky and received the revelation. She did not have to die. That was not in God's plan. He prayed and the Lord brought back the woman to life.

The Lord Jesus still operates miracles today and all those who trust completely in him to become his disciples experiment divine intervention. He also does miracles which will constitute a judgment for those who benefit from them and do not decide to walk in his ways.

Georgette is a young lady who had never failed at school until she entered the university. After numerous failures at her university studies, she started wondering why she was failing. She realized that, in her family, no one had a university diploma, despite their high intellectual level. She received the revelation that a curse had been placed upon her family and because of which no one would ever get a diploma beyond the GCE diploma level. She then turned towards Jesus with all her heart, who led her to professional studies. Without any other failure, she got her BTS (Brevet d'Etudes Supérieures), and the following year, she got a professional BA (Licence) in Advertisement.

Here is another testimony. There is a woman who was divorced and who had left the city where her husband lived for quite a number of years. One day, she became delivered after several prayer sessions of deliverance. Because of her attachment to the word of God, she became delivered from the demons of rejection, from physical degradation and from all the spirits which had been let loose in her through occult traditional customs. When she obtained her deliverance, she completely changed: her face became younger instantly. Upon seeing her, one would not take her for the same woman she previously was. She even became more beautiful. The pastor advised her to go back to her husband (as the Lord hates divorce (Mal.2:16). Pastor Emmanuel Kom accompanied her to her husband. He was delighted to see how her husband welcomed her. It is as if he did not recognize her. When she

67

told him her name, he was astounded as he saw her so beautiful and shining. Since that day, she remains with her husband and they enjoy their marriage entirely as husband and wife.

The following testimony is that of Moussa Kone who received the visitation of Jesus Christ in person. Moussa Kone, a son of an Imam, had been initiated while still young to Islam, to the reading of the Koran. At the age of fourteen, he was able to read the Koran perfectly to the extent that he could teach it to other children of his quarter, and to bring the children of different ethnic groups to Islam.

One day, while reading the Koran with his father, he asked him one question that came to his mind: "if today we were to die, shall we both go the paradise?"

His father gave him a sincere response: "My son, I do not know. And I cannot know because the Koran does not say it clearly." The response disturbed him, but it did not change his attitude with respect to the study of the Koran. At the age of eighteen years old, he could accomplish so many things thanks by merely reciting the Suras of the Koran. For his initiation to become a "marabout," one night, around 2am, at the present location of the Société Ivoirienne de Raffinerie, while he was sitting with his father and one his father's friends, in the bush, he was reciting Yassim's Sura. Ten minutes later, a strange being appeared. His father's friend went aside to talk to this being for about 20 to 30 minutes. That being was a spirit that came to make an appointment with them.

The following day, at 4PM, the three of them were meeting in a courtyard that was completely locked, and they had in front of them a big suitcase. They started reciting the Suras at the end of which they were mentioning the name of a city and bank notes of a thousand francs CFA fell from above. The money was probably coming from the banks of Cote d'Ivoire. That is probably why the bank tellers of these banks often have problems with their company. Another event that took place is that of a teacher who liked a white woman; he came to obtain a talisman. He asked him a grey hair (cheveux de blanc) and made something called 'kawatin', a technique that consists of changing a name into numbers and to put them in a square in a given order, then one wraps the whole thing in leather or in another object that is given back to the customer. He made a liquid from this technique on the walaha (a wooden slate) and gave it to him as a perfume (baume). He then changed their name into a number in the square, put all of it in a given order and wrote the name of Mohammed on the four sides. Three months after this, they got married. Today, this family has a lot of problems and that man is miserable. The power of the demon has an end whereas that of God is unlimited, he said to himself.

Despite all this knowledge he had, that question that he had asked of his father often came back to his mind. Although he lived in relative joy, the financial difficulties of his father pushed him to seek a job and work. He found a job as a sailor on a boat called Grand Bassam, which was an American platform. He worked in the sea for eight years. It was during those eight years that he lived the most extraordinary experiences with the Lord. One evening, Mr. Welford, the boat captain, came to his cabin to talk to him. He was surprised because this boat captain was a special authority. This boat captain came at the time when he was reading the Koran. He had his Bible in one of his hands. The captain told him that he came to talk to him about Jesus. Suddenly, Moussa became so angry because the mere mention of Jesus irritated him. He took the Bible that the captain had put on his bed and threw it into the sea. That action assuaged him as he thought he had hurt the boat captain's self esteem. When he turned towards him, he was disconcerted to see a big smile on the lips of this Christian. Then the boat captain told him calmly: "cool down, my boy".

"You know that I am Muslim and Mohammed is my prophet. Allah is my God. If you do it again, I will just get out of your boat."

But the boat captain did not get angry. He refrained from talking to him about Jesus Christ directly. He did not get discouraged. It was even at that time that their relation got closer. At times, he offered him non alcoholic drinks when it was hot and helped him with the machines. Later on, he allowed himself to talk about the Koran with a Ghanaian who spoke Arabic perfectly. The question that he had once asked of his father kept coming back to his mind. He decided to look further into the Koran in order to find the answer to that question and verses that would demonstrate that the Bible was falsified.

As he progressively studied the Koran while devoting this endeavor to God, he realized that he was not saved and that he was a sinner. The Koran stipulates the following: "you will certainly see hell and you will have to account for your good acts on this earth." No doubt then that he would be precipitated in hell. He was beset by anxiety at the idea that he would meet in hell the thugs of Abidjan who knew him and who would laugh at him.

That day, he closed the Koran and slept with fear in his heart. In the Koran, the 2nd Sura, verse 130 that he read the following day, said the following:

70

"Proclaim that we believe in God, it is God who revealed himself to Abraham, Isaac, and to the twelve tribes of Israel, to Moses and to Jesus". Note that the book of Moses is the Pentateuch and the one of Jesus is the Injil (Gospel). He read again in the Koran: "after the other prophets, we sent Jesus, the son of Mary with the Gospel, confirming what is in the Pentateuch, and the Gospel is the direction and the light for all the people (5th Sura, verse 50). Those who hold the Gospel judge according to its contents and the one who does not judge according to the book of God is astray." He thus understood that anyone who directs his life according to the Gospel is directed by God. He then started wondering: "if God has sent his word through the Gospel, why would he send another word that is contradictory? From what I know, the Koran and the Bible are opposed. How come that God who is straight and just could have done that!" He also found in the Koran passages such as the following (cf. Sura 19, verses 16,17): "We sent our spirit who took a human form in front of Miryam (Mary) [...] in order to announce the arrival of the holy Child"; contrary to Mohammed who is the son of Abdallah, Jesus is called the apostle of God, the spirit of God, one of the relatives of God who is honored on earth and beyond. Unlike the man who, upon his death, goes back to ashes, when Jesus died, he went back to God and not to ashes. He thus admitted that Jesus is far superior to a human being since all the other prophets had sins that they had to confess, including Mohammed.

Moreover, there are contradictions in the Koran, he noticed, at different levels. It said that Mohammed is the greatest prophet, but also that Jesus was not dead, but that someone else had been substituted to him according to God's plan (Sura 4, verse 156). Obviously, this verse contradicted

71

Sura 3, verse 55: "Oh Jesus, I will make you experience death, I will raise you to me, I will deliver you from the infidels and those who will follow in your footsteps will be above those who do not believe in you." He felt as if he was just shot down by that verse. He analyzed that verse and said to himself that "I will make you experience death, this resembles crucifixion, and I will raise you to me, which refers to the resurrection". He was convinced and he had always been convinced that Jesus was not dead and that the crucifixion and the resurrection that Christians talk about were lies, according to the teachings that they had received. That is how Moussa found himself facing truth in the Koran. That truth, he found its confirmation in Sura 19, verse 34: "Jesus while he was still very young in his manger said: peace will be upon me the day I will be born, the day I will die, and the day I will resuscitate." This really convinced him. He understood a number of things in six months.

Throughout the various contradictions about Jesus in the Koran, passages do confirm the veracity of the Bible. He thus became convinced that: there was no salvation in the Koran, the Bible is confirmed by the Koran, Jesus is above all the other prophets, he is the Messiah, the apostle of God, the son of Mary, the Spirit coming from God, the word of God, one of God's confident, honored down here on earth and beyond. After that discovery, he no longer knew what to do; he tried to get out, he was unable to eat. He became morose because he knew that he was not saved.

That evening, he vowed to himself: "if this test comes from God, let him prove it to me physically and let him show me what I ought to do." As he went back home (that is back to his cabin), he talked to God, no longer in Arabic, but in his mother tongue, the Dioula: "My father is an Imam. When I am with him, I direct the prayer. All my uncles are Imams. I am a descendant of an Imam. I cannot therefore abandon Islam."

He switched off the lights and, suddenly, another light appeared in his cabin. Someone was there. At first, he got frightened. But soon after, he overcame his fear. That person came forward and put his hand on his right hand shoulder. He began to talk to him. And then, suddenly, everything became dark. He looked for that being everywhere in his cabin but he could not find him. He was unable to sleep all night long. The following morning, he took the Koran and recited the Yassim Sura. He did not know that he was thus challenging God. Suddenly, he saw an ember on the right page of his Koran. Before he could even make up his mind on what to do, another ember appeared. There were a lot of them. The Koran began to burn. He was scared because the holy book of the whole Islam, of every Muslim that he was holding in his hand was burning. He spent four nights without sleeping because he resisted falling asleep. When he finally fell asleep, he saw a tall man who was standing in front of him. He was ready to touch him. He refused to identify himself. He then started to recite the credo of Islam, then he stepped back and disappeared. He understood that it was Islam that was abandoning him for ever. When he landed at Cocody, he found the missionary with whom he had discussed earlier and he told him that he had just accepted Jesus Christ. Then they prayed together. Today Moussa Kone is a pastor who directs the assemblies and goes around the world proclaiming the good news of the kingdom of God.

He had needed divine intervention to bring him the assurance of salvation. He discovered that salvation can only be found in Jesus Christ.

There is also this story of a city gangster who got shot just under his navel while he was trying to escape from the site of the crime. The police brought him to a local hospital under their surveillance. His wound got worse and worse. He was then abandoned in his room with this open wound on his stomach.

A few days later, his mother came to see him and talk to him about God's love through Christ. As he was stubborn, he found himself alone pondering about his destiny after his mother left. Soon after this, he entered into a comatose state. That is when he got this vision that was going to completely change his life.

That evening, he saw a cross covered with blood coming towards him. He got utterly frightened. When the cross reached him, he saw a drop of blood trickle from it and rest on him. Suddenly, a powerful glare from nowhere completely covered him. That is how he came out of this comatose state and his open wound which was already infected progressively healed without any medication whatsoever.

He decided to completely devote his life to his savior. Since then, he started spending his time in prison praising God's wonders and studying the Bible. As soon as he got released from jail, he enrolled in a Biblical school with the help of Christians.

Today, the Lord uses him to enable paralytics to walk, the blind to see and the sick to recover merely through prayers. The Lord has literally changed him so much that his life is so exemplary to the extent that his relatives who had already rejected him now welcome him wholeheartedly.

Several people, upon listening to his preaching the Gospel, have been taking the firm decision to repent in order to live according to the divine principles of the Bible.

Finally, God intervened in the life of three sisters in an extraordinary manner. One evening, there was an outage in the city of Bertoua. In the house of an evangelical missionary, the housekeeper lit a candle that he put on the floor in the corridor before going to bed. He was the last to go to bed and he forgot to extinguish the candle. A thick smoke woke them up in the middle of the night. They wanted to rush outside into the corridor to see what was happening. As soon as each of them, including their father who was in his room, opened the door that exits to the corridor, they were greeted by thick flames. This instantly pushed them to close the door immediately. They tried to undo the anti-theft metal frames on the windows in order to escape. The neighbors came to help them. These anti-theft metal frames were solidly attached to the wall, it was impossible to remove them. The more time passed, the more desperate they were for escaping. The missionary who was also their father saw that a gas bottle was in his room. For the sake of preserving his family, he took his courage in his hands, opened the door and rolled the gas bottle in the flames in the corridor until the exit. His son, through a sheer act of bravery, opened the door and rushed to the exit. He too was seriously burnt and his state was very critical. The three sisters who were in their room tried to open the door but the flame was so gigantic that they could not face it. They told themselves that this was their end, and that, before they depart from this world, as good Christians, they had to examine their lives and confess all their sins and repent. After doing that, they started praising the Lord. It would be good to go to the Father in heaven while praising him. They were worshiping and praising the Lord when they heard a big noise from the other side of the door, in the corridor, at the location where the flames were raging.

Suddenly, the door opened. A giant man was standing by the door and was blocking the flames. He asked them to get out. There was something like a second passage in the corridor, inside the flames, a passage without any flame which had been extraordinarily isolated. The three sisters went out one after the other. People were very surprised to see them getting out through the flames without any burning, safe and sane. Only one of them had a scratch on the door because she had rushed while going out. That evening, they told everybody who asked them questions what had happened. But they could not find their benefactor. He had disappeared. They then understood that that man had been an angel sent by God. They had never seen him before. After getting out of the house, they no longer saw him. The house burnt completely. The father and the boy who had acted heroically, while forgetting to confide themselves in God, came out rather sad. They succumbed to their wounds. That is how the three sisters miraculously escaped from death that would have been caused by arson and they were able to give the testimony that God operated a miracle in their lives.

All these testimonies stand as a living proof that God that we serve through Jesus Christ is simply omnipotent. He is really the almighty. Nothing is above his power. It is our iniquities which create a separation between him and us. He allowed Kone to find him because Kone looked for him with all his heart. Even today, he still resuscitates the dead. There is no disease whatsoever that God cannot cure in the name of Jesus. He is the one who breaks the curses of all those who are tied to him with a repenting heart and who are ready to receive him at the mention of the name of Jesus.

As I finished reading all these testimonies, I had a feeling of admiration for Gaelle. There are times, I was worried that her testimony about the Muslims would be dangerous as it is the type of testimony that certain Muslims may not accept. At the same time, I was amazed in the way she was using the Koran, citing specific passages in the Suras to prove the veracity of the Bible. I told myself that our Muslim friends ought to read them and decide for themselves on the value of what Gaelle had written. If she is correct that Pastor Kone whose tale she is recounting in this testimony, was truly the son of an Imam, then certainly there must be something right in what he was saying. We will never know how the Lord God judges us, that is, how he judges Christians, Muslims, Buddhists, and so on. What I am sure of is that there is always a divine bud that lies in people of all faiths and when people behave in accordance with this divine bud, God will always be sensitive to their requests.

As I even thought further about it, I toyed with the idea that, maybe, upon reading Gaelle's testimony, Muslims and Christians will realize that they worship the same God after all. I wondered how the Imams would interpret the text. Could they take the lead to instruct their flocks that Muslims all over the world must accept Jesus Christ as not merely a prophet, but as the true son of God? The burning of the Koran could then be interpreted as the manifestation of God's anger towards people who oppose his will. From a strictly personal point of view, I must confess that I very much admire the Muslims as I see them pray five times a day, observe the Ramadan, wake up everyday very early in the morning to go to the mosque, and so on. Were they to accept Jesus Christ as the son of God, I hope they would keep their strong faith in God and continue to worship him as honestly and sincerely as they can. At the same time, I feel that the Muslim youth would feel much happier if they were to really worship God without having to do it as a burden imposed by their religion. Respecting fasting during the Ramadan would then be done out of conviction. They would be allowed to mix with Christians to deepen their faith as they would know that they are worshiping the same God with their fellow Christians. In the end, Christians and Muslims would hopefully belong to this "universal church" and truly live as brothers and sisters because that is ultimately God's will.

In the following testimonies, we will see another type of realities, this time related to witchcraft. Here again, we will see that God intervenes in his own way to save the children who ask his help.

Chapter 6

Rescue from Witchcraft

In my sociolinguistics class, there are students who seem to relate to me, not as a teacher, but as a friend. One such girl is Sigue Carlise Lydie. One can see that she does not come from a wealthy family. Her behavior shows that she is simple, much like the way our own Georgina was. When she heard that my daughter died, she also came to convey her condolences. As I talked to her, I discovered that, in her childhood, she had lived a difficult life because she grew up in a milieu infested by witchcraft. In addition, she did not really live with her two parents. It is amazing that she looks a well balanced lady and I really pray that she will be succeeding in her life. What she tells us in her written testimony is a reminder that, like Marietou said in her poem, we are a miracle. We have perhaps been born in a good family and we have grown without facing problems that millions of other individuals face. Just as Georgina noticed that her handicap was not the worst when she saw other handicapped children in Ghana, we should always thank God that he has perhaps given us a body, a family, a social context in which he wanted us to bloom. Here is Sigue's written testimony (the original is written in French, so this is my translation).

She entitled her paper as: *God's divine intervention in our life.*

The world today is not like the world in the past. Satan has taken the upper hand on the world and he constantly sinks God's creatures in all sorts of evil deeds. His goal is for us not to live in the ways of our Lord, but rather to find our way towards his own abode, that is, hell. As human beings are under the domination of the devil, they do all sorts of debauchery, and they thus put their lives and their neighbors' lives into great peril. How does a human being succeed to overcome this situation? It is in a bid to answer that question that I will present my own testimony and that of my father in this squib.

I grew up at my granny's in a small town of Melong that is located in the Moungo division. In my quarter, our nearest neighbor who was about sixty-five years old did not have any child. When I was five years old, I only lived with my grandmother and my aunt and I used to go and play in the playground of my neighbor until the day I unearthed, unwillingly, a bottle of medication (fetishes) that this woman had buried in front of her door. As I was going towards our house to show it to my grandmother, this woman came to grab me from behind, and then snatched the bottle from me and started heaping insult on me. I can no longer remember the exact wording of those insults except the words "bad pikin," in Pidgin English, which literally means "bad child." I thus went back home crying and I explained it to my grandmother what had just occurred to me. Since that day, this neighbor started to hate me. Each time she saw me, her face turned morose and she would then spit as if she had seen a pile of feces. In addition, she always tried to create trouble with my grandmother who prayed a lot so as not to succumb to her provocations.

To tell the truth, I never believed in witchcraft until the day I got to form one of elementary school. Two weeks before the exam, I fell sick and it was that woman who was threatening me every night. Whenever I slept, someone always appeared in front of me and I was unable to describe him/her and to unveil who it was. I was really threatened. I felt fever all over my body but everyone thought this was due to the stress caused by the exam. One week before the GCE O level (probatoire), my sickness got worse. I swallowed drugs, but they did not relieve me. My grandmother who was a fervent Christian full of faith began to pray for me. Then she would make me lick olive oil that has been blessed. During the prayers, I felt the sickness go away from me and, by the grace of God, I passed my GCE O level exam.

In my last year of high school, I became ill again two weeks before the exam. This time, the sickness was worse and my family wept. As God is so merciful, he opened my eyes to what was really happening in my life. One night, I realized that it was my neighbor who was haunting me again. My sickness was so terrible that I had to sleep with my mother. One evening, I really saw death in my own eyes and the following day, my grandmother was to go for a trip. Around 3AM, she entered my room to check on me and say goodbye. I was literally burning. We were waiting for daylight in order for me to be brought to the hospital. When my grandmother left the room, I saw my neighbor appear in white. I got a slap from her on my cheek. That is when I realized that I was the only one to see her and to hear her. After slapping me, she went out by the door. Tears were flowing from my eyes and I was unable to make any noise. I could no longer speak and my limbs could no longer move. I was totally unable to inform my mother or to wake her up. I knew that was the end for me: I was merely waiting for my death. Fortunately for me, God came to my help. I suddenly felt that my arms were no longer tied, and I was able to open my mouth and tell my mother what had just happened to me. Panic settled in. However, we both prayed and I felt a bit relieved. Early in the morning, my mother wanted to bring me to hospital but I refused because I knew that my disease was mystical and that only God would be the one to cure me through prayers. I took a machete and went out to fight this evil wizard who wanted to kill me. Fortunately for her, she stayed locked inside her house. Everybody was amazed to find me in such a state, as they had seen how sick I was the previous day. I simply told them that my God had cured me without telling them what really happened lest they be tempted to threaten me.

At the end of that scene, my family and I prayed. My grandmother gave me some blessed water that I poured everywhere in my room. Following her instructions, I ate some jujube seeds and took some ash inside the palm of my hand and then I blew it from the kitchen to the verandah while asking the wizard to leave me in peace. Thanks to God, I recovered and obtained my GCE A level diploma.

As for the second testimony, I must state first that life is full of surprises and whatever happens to us derives from the will of God. This is a testimony of my father who has often recounted it to me with tears in his eyes.

My father met my mother when he was twenty-six years old. My mother already had two children with another man who had abandoned her, but my father loved her and both of them lived in perfect harmony and love. My mother was a housewife and my father a cashier in a bakery in the town of Melong where I was born.

People envied the couple and were jealous as they could not understand how an abandoned woman with two children could have found a husband who was so good. It is true that both of them were not married yet, but part of the dowry had already been paid. It is also true that both were extremely pretentious and open minded to the extent that they forgot that man is jealous by nature, especially when he feels inferior, or when he realizes that he cannot get what his neighbor has got in abundance, or simply because he is proud and that the only thing he can do is to strike in order for the other person to open for him.

My father used to share a lot but he did not know that this was dangerous for him. His life became sour when a colleague of his stole a sum of 200,000 CFA francs. The jealous co-workers went to see the director of the bakery, that is, the boss, and they accused my father as the culprit. Through God's intervention, I might say, the bandit who had stolen the money denounced himself but the boss got manipulated by these jealous coworkers who declared at the tribunal that my father had been in connivance with the bandit. This boss of the bakery who was an influential personality in the city led the affair to the tribunal of Nkongsamba.

My father got dismissed and began to live in real hell. He was no longer able to pay the rent, in short, he could not make the two ends meet. As a solution, he decided to go and leave my mother and his furniture at my grandmother's place as she inhabited the same city. Her house was empty and he was sleeping on cardboards in the living room. He literally became an object of mockery. All his clothes were with my grandmother and that is where he usually went to change himself. At that time, I was a fetus because my mother was three-months pregnant.

Now that my mother was alone on her side, she succumbed to the machinations of the jealous coworkers who told him that my father had stolen the amount of money he was accused of. One should note that, as my mother was materialistic and that she was pressured by the manipulations of the jealous coworkers, she ended up changing the love she had for my father into hatred. She no longer wanted to see him and whenever he came to our house, she would welcome him by heaping insults on him. As my father did not know what else he could do, and which saint to invoke, he simply went back to his parents at Nkongsamba where he lived a real Calvary.

His parents did not accept him. They told him that he no longer had a place in their house. They insulted him, cursed him by telling him that he went to spend the money with a prostitute (that is, my mother) who must have ruined him and chased him. My father cried everyday and he had only a single cloth that he washed and dried each time he came back from the tribunal. He saw his life crumbling just like a cattle of cards.

In the meantime, I was growing inside the womb of my mother who no longer loved my father. He was now abandoned and the only consolation he received was from his elder sister who used to give him sleeping pills to help him sleep. She is the one who sometimes gave him food and invited him to her bar to make him breathe fresh air and forget his despicable situation.

My father stayed at home almost naked because it was crucial that he keep his pants and shirt for his appointment at the tribunal. His parents were indifferent and used to heap insults on him. Thanks to God's grace, my father found a lawyer who pleaded for him and won the trial. He was to benefit from a large amount of money for winning the trial, but the judge was soon bribed by the director of the bakery who was very influential and well known in the area.

Meanwhile, my mother gave birth to me. My father was informed because he always cared to seek information about me and wanted very much to see me. When he arrived at my grandmother's place, my mother had already brought me to Douala. My father then sent his elder sister to go and look for me in Douala as my mother was already working in a local fishery. As soon as my mother got informed of this, she sent me to Yaounde to live with her uncle until I became five years old. It is only then that I went back to Melong to live with my grandmother, and thus continue living without paternal affection.

My father was jobless. His life was very monotonous. Everyday, he walked around looking for menial jobs. He sometimes found them in carpentry and on building sites. Once he was hired, he used to work like a real slave but he was always badly paid because his salary was 500 CFA francs per day, but it was better than nothing.

One day, as he was walking, he entered an apostolic church. He attended the church service and he liked it. He went there every Sunday to pray. His state and character attracted the attention of several parishioners, most particularly that of a rich female deacon to whom my father recounted the saga of his past. My father was really interested to hear the word of God. He wanted to serve God but he did not have any money to attend a theological school. Fortunately, God used this woman to open him the door that leads to him. That woman accepted to take care of everything and she did it during the last two years that preceded her death. My father did not believe that he would still continue his studies after this lady's death, but God never closes a door without opening another. Given the fact that the training lasted three years, my father had to spend one more year in order to become a pastor. This time, God helped him through an elder of the apostolic church to open him the door. It was almost unbelievable for my father to witness this miracle he was living in his miserable life. He faithfully pursued his training and was ordained pastor of the apostolic church in 1996, thanks to God's intervention who never forgets his children. For my father, this was just a dream come true. Given his past, he could not believe that he was now an ordained pastor.

By that time, I was twelve years old and my grandmother took good care of me to the extent that I was not beset by any worries. However, I sometimes asked her who was my father and she always answered me that it is my grandfather who was my father. As I thought about it, I could never bring myself to accept that my grandmother's husband who was also the father of my aunt with whom I was staying would also be my father. I knew that there was something wrong. At times, my grandmother would show me a picture and she would tell me that it was my father as if she was kidding. And yet, it was true.

I was in fifth form when, for the first time, I received a man and a woman who brought me greetings from my father. I was surprised and did not know which father they were talking about. As my grandfather had just died, I told them that I no longer have a father and then they went away, disappointed.

Several months went by. One day, while I was cooking, the youngest brother of my father arrived, and he told me that my father wanted him to greet me and inquire about my whereabouts. From that day, I understood that my father was alive and that he missed me. I began to pray so that God may help me to find him because I started feeling that I also missed him a lot. God heeded my prayers after two years, that is, while I was in form 3. One evening, I was at home alone. There was an outage and I was sitting on the verandah in complete darkness when a man arrived and called me by my name. I was very surprised because I had never seen him. Fortunately, he had torchlight. We then went in the living room. I was very afraid of this stranger, who happened to be my father. I then remembered that he called me by my name and I thus had the feeling that the stranger who was in front of me was my father. I was impatient to discover his face and it is as if God was reading my thoughts. Two minutes later, the lights came on but I did not have the courage to look at him in the eyes. My father was talking to me with a trembling voice when my mother and my grandmother entered the living room and called him by his praise name.

I thought I was dreaming but it was sheer reality. It was a great joy at home because, thanks to God's grace, the child and the father had reunited. Today, I "worship" my father and sometimes ask myself what I would have become if I never knew him.

It is well known that the human being has been created in the image of God and that he was called upon to dominate the whole world. Today, there are many people who are real demons and who find pleasure in causing trouble to their neighbor. As a matter of fact, when a person faces all sorts of dangers, he feels obliged to call on God the father for help. God always answers this call for those who do it in great faith. The paradox is that, even the evil people, before they do evil or when they feel in danger, they also call on God. This is a further proof of God's power as the creator, his ability to resolve any kind of problem and to save our life.

The time of God is the best. One just has to be patient because he never forgets his children.

I would like to add a personal note to Sigue Carlise's remark that evildoers also invoke God. This is true, indeed. At times, one even has the impression that God heeds their prayers. I have recently heard of a woman who is a specialist in child trafficking from Africa to Europe. One day, she was arrested at the Roissy Charles de Gaulle airport of Paris. She had four children that she was trying to infiltrate into France. For the first time, she realized that she was caught at last in her illegal game and that she would certainly be jailed. She started praying thus: "My God, you know that I always pay my tithes to the church. You also know that I do not like to see people suffering. I always endeavor to help them. Do not abandon me at this critical moment." Soon after this prayer, a female customs officer called her into her office and asked her whether the four children in her passport were really her children. She said yes. She knew that she was telling a lie. Curiously enough, the customs officer gave her back her passport and allowed her to continue her trip, that is, to bring the four children to France. She interpreted this as a miracle originating from God. I also know a state employee who is among the few beneficiaries of huge amounts of money in an African country. One day, a general in the army was appointed as his boss. Unfortunately, he wanted to sack him from his job. Following what he told us, he started praying and fasting as he was a fervent follower of the Virgin Mary. He told us that the Virgin Mary must have intervened for him because he not only succeeded to keep his job, but he also became promoted to a better position. I also know several people who seemingly benefit from God's abundant grace, but when you scrutinize their lives, you discover that their style of living does not reflect God's will at all. Some practice abortions without resenting any kind of remorse, others use their positions as priests or pastors to make more money for their personal needs, sometimes, through illegal means. Since this book is about the divine bud, I believe we should never interpret what might appear as God's intervention as evidence that He approves our evil deeds. To me, it is possible that the evil spirit may be the origin of what might appear as God's intervention but which, as a matter of fact, is a means to waylay people and prevent them from following the narrow path that leads to God. It is up to us to detect Satan's machinations and thus implore God's divine mercy. As I have said earlier, upon our death, God will ask us to account for our deeds. Therefore, we should not lure ourselves into practicing evil deeds while imploring God as if He approved them.

Chapter 7

Other Miraculous Testimonies

To a certain extent, I have to recognize that what I saw as God's intervention in Georgina's life made me discover other facets of my sociolinguistics class. Although, as the teacher, I am the eldest, I realized that I am not the wisest, especially in religious matters. I even have to reveal that I felt far less experienced than most of my students. When they tell about their private lives, they have so many interesting stories to reveal. For the time being, I would like to concentrate on one of the students whose name is Jean Patrick.

This is a boy who is relatively brilliant, who always makes an effort to work well. But, at the same time, like most of my students, I could not say that he was totally committed to his studies. Sometimes, he would be absent. And believe me, when he was absent, there was always a reason. As we started talking about the possible papers we could write in honor of Georgina's memory, I discovered that Jean Patrick was a professional pastor. I must also reveal that he reminded me of another friend of mine who is a pastor. His name is Rudolphe Melingui. He is a former colonel of the Cameroonian army. He is now retired but he was very active in so many things. I hope I will have the opportunity of coming back to him some time later in this book.

Let me just give you the text that Jean Patrick wrote, in French, as his testimonies before I make a few more comments on him.

The scientific world is really complicated. It always remains skeptical towards the religious issues. It consists mostly of people who rarely believe that God takes care of human beings by intervening in their lives. It seems therefore important to bring some light to this issue so that the scientific community may take seriously the action of God in our lives. In this squib, I propose five testimonies likely to contribute to draw their interest to this issue.

My first testimony took place in 1997 when I was merely 13 years old. I distinctly experimented the action of God in the life of my father whose name is Mve Esso Jean, a former school teacher. While he was working on the playground in the village, he became a victim of a spell. As he commented, "as I touched the handles of the wheelbarrow I was using to collect the garbage, I fell as if I was electrocuted, and suddenly, a fire lit up inside my stomach." I personally witnessed the evolution of my father's suffering. The man that I knew as a very valiant individual, stout and practicing sports, had become very weak, very slim, and what is worse, he became unable to walk two meters without taking a rest. Furthermore, he began to move while screaming, with the help of a stick to support him.

One day, my elder brother Narcisse who was already a Christian brought my father to his pastor, (Reverend Evangelist Jean C. at Sangmelima, our native city. Thus, after talking to my father about God, the man of God prayed for him. Soon after this, my father threw away his walking stick and began to walk normally. Even the fire that used to burn inside his stomach stopped and everything came back to normal. This is how my father whose death everybody was expecting in the village returned there in good form while giving thanks to the Lord God who had intervened in his life.

He resumed his activities, such as his work in his farms, as usual.

The second testimony that made me witness the action of God in our lives also took place in 1997. This testimony is about an elder cousin of mine, Andrew, who lived in the village. Andrew had a house but he never lived inside it because of threats that he usually experimented there. As he usually reported, "whenever I stayed in my house, I would see a casket that came to land in front of me and opened so that I may enter it. Moreover, I used to see in my dreams people who requested me to sleep inside that casket." What happens is that he had indeed practiced black magic when he was young and he had received material and money that came from the mystical world. People from that mystical world were thus requesting him a ransom by offering his own life. As a consequence, he fled his house and stayed at a neighbor's place. His house has remained haunted for several years.

One day, an evangelization campaign took place in Oveng-Yemvak, my village. Andrew, whose house was haunted, confided himself to the Lord God and presented him his problem by explaining it to the pastor. This pastor went to pray in the haunted house and it became a normal and habitable house again. Thus, thanks to the action of God, Andrew lives in his house today.

The third testimony took place in 2003. Again, I experimented the manifestation of God's power through his action in the life of the Evangelist Jean Claude, who was a native of the Center province that I mentioned above. Jean Claude had been poisoned in the village while he was conducting an evangelization campaign. He went to different hospitals where he was told that his case was very serious.

Several treatments were tried but in vain. His situation was even becoming worse and worse. He had become much blacker than he was before, with an expanded (bloated) stomach, and he became unable to defecate. As you know, this kind of poisoning very often leads to death.

However, one day, fervent Christians of his community began to pray God for him and everything that was in his stomach got out. That is how he got delivered through the action of God our creator, and today, he continues to preach the Gospel of the Lord and to exert his function of provincial pedagogic inspector.

The fourth testimony concerns me. My name is Mve Jean Patrick, a native of the Dja and Lobo subdivision in the south Province of Cameroon. What happened soon after I obtained my GCE (Baccalauréat) diploma, I went to enroll at the University of Yaounde 1, more precisely in 2005. Everything seemed to be going very well for me. I did not know that I was already a victim of jealousy, and on the rebound, a victim of witchcraft practice in the village. Thus, soon after the beginning of the courses in October 2005, I was taken ill. At first, we thought that is was malaria. I was then submitted to a treatment at the first-aid post of "la Montée des Soeurs" here in Yaounde. After undergoing several drips, it was obvious that I was not going to recover. I lost all my energy and became paralyzed at the level of my back. I could no longer lie down and something was gnawing my left-hand lung. I was then transferred to Jamot hospital. Later on, I underwent a surgical operation and other laboratory tests at the Centre Pasteur of Yaounde.

After all these maneuvers, that is, the surgical operation, radiography, lab tests, unclear results, treatment, etc., the situation was even becoming worse. I really could feel my death approaching in big strides. My present pastor began to pray for me. After that, one day, while I was alone in my room, a shining light descended upon me, enveloped all my body and it enabled me to sleep very profoundly. The following morning, when I woke up, I fell in good health: I was full of energy, I was no longer paralyzed, in short, God had saved me from death which was about to engulf my life.

Curiously enough, when I went to the village during the Christmas holidays, everybody who saw me told me this: "we were only expecting your remains (corpse) and your casket here at the village." I was greatly surprised because no one had ever informed people in the village about my sickness. As you can see, today I am alive thanks to the grace of God and I pursue my studies in Masters I at the Department of African languages and linguistics here at the University of Yaounde 1.

The last testimony is an event that occurred in 2007 and it is related to the life on my friend Patrick Nodier of the West province of Cameroon. He has a Masters degree in chemistry. One day, he went to a church of which I am a member. His goal was merely to talk to the pastor. During the talk, he declared to the pastor that there was no longer any reason for him to live and that he wanted to make suicide. Indeed, he had been diagnosed as being HIV positive. This is what he told the pastor:

"I did a first lab test that turned out positive, then I did a second one with the same positive results. This means that I am HIV positive. My studies will go to the drain and I must end up dying very soon."

The pastor preached him the Gospel and told him that God could change everything in his life. He accepted to believe in God, and then soon after giving him pieces of advice, the pastor prayed for him. One of the following days, the pastor asked him to go and do another lab test. When he did it, the results were negative. He then did a fourth test with the same negative results. He had become HIV-negative again. He went back to the church and thanked God who had just cured him from AIDS. Today, we live together and Nodier is alive today in good health thanks to God's intervention.

What we should ultimately retain from these testimonies is that God truly acts in our lives. These testimonies constitute irrefutable proof of God's divine intervention in our lives. However, it is necessary to note that, for this intervention to manifest its effects, this must be the result of deep faith in God. To say it differently, it is only fervent faith to God that produces such results.

As I read these messages, I now understood why Jean Patrick was so committed to serving God and why his classmates called him a pastor. It looks like he is a real pastor, but I could not understand why a pastor would be taking regular courses at the university instead of staying in his church, preaching the word of God. In one of my private encounters with him, I asked him if he was a real pastor. He said that he is not ordained yet and that he works under the supervision of a Bamileke pastor. He hopes to become nonetheless an ordained pastor.

What really convinced me that he may be a real pastor is that, in class, we had so many questions about people who get possessed or who are bewitched by mystical powers. Jean Patrick was able to tell us how to deal with such people. He said that, demons have various powers. There are demons that might have ten different powers, others six, and others two. You have to know how to deal with such demons. And if your faith is not deep enough, even if you are a pastor, you might end up harming yourself as you try to fight such demons. For certain demons, to get rid of them, you need to fast even for a number of days before proceeding to the deliverance ceremony. Upon hearing how he could give detailed explanations how to get rid of demons, I really believed that he is a man of God, the expression he likes to use when speaking about pastors or evangelists.

As I thought about the lively intervention Jean Patrick did in class and that convinced me that he is truly a man of God, I asked him to write down the quintessence of that intervention and that, if I find it satisfactory, I may integrate it in our *Divine Bud* book. This is what he then wrote. (Again, the original text is in French).

The men of God have always been interested in the well-being of the populations. That is why various problems of a spiritual or biological nature are often submitted to them. Spiritually, the cases are most of the time related to possessions, bewitchment, and haunting. Biologically, the cases are usually related to blindness, deafness, blockage, poisoning, paralysis, epilepsy, madness, sterility; eventually, one may come across various other cases such as HIV/AIDS, cancer, malaria, and so on. For the men of God, it is often imperative to counteract these multiple evils by praying for the victims. They thus proceed to deliverances and to chasing away the demons (the evil spirits). The main objective here is to show to people that God acts and intervenes in our lives.

Yet, very often, not all men of God are successful in this enterprise. There are pastors who cannot even pray in order to deliver someone from a simple headache or a simple toothache. On the other hand, there are men of God who pray and the seropositive become seronegative, the blind recover their sight, the lepers become pure, and the paralytics walk. Some other pastors pray and the dead resuscitate. This difference among the servants of God in the process of conducting deliverance sessions is manifested day in and day out in our societies.

One can thus find someone possessed who has not been delivered at a pastor's church. But, when another pastor prays for him, the demons that possess him flee instantly. We even witness cases where some exorcists are attacked by the bad spirits when they want to start the deliverance sessions. Some of them even become crazy. One event that took place in Ezeka, a small town between Yaounde and Lolodorf, is a case in point. In this town, there was a man whose house was haunted by demoniac powers. Two pastors whose names I do not wish to disclose decided to go and pray in order to put an end to this haunting. As they got to the house, one of the pastors got attacked by the demons and he suddenly collapsed. It became thus necessary for the other pastor to first pray for his colleague before chasing away the evil spirits from that haunted house.

When facing such situations, one often wonders what may be the cause. In other words, is there a magic formula that some pastors use to chase away demons and that other pastors ignore? We [meaning probably I and other pastors] believe and we know that there is no magic formula in this enterprise. There are just a number of things you need to understand. First, one has to be called or chosen by God as

98

his servant; in other words, one should not proclaim himself as a man of God, or eventually pursue some training as a pastor because one has been failing in his worldly endeavors and he thus hopes that, by becoming a pastor, he will be successful.

Secondly, a servant of God who wants to be powerful should not live like other people: he must avoid sins at all costs. It is often observed that a pastor who is guilty of the following sins is not likely to deliver a patient from his problems: lying, adultery, impudicity, theft, hatred, corruption and other various sins. Another obstacle that would render the men of God impotent in conducting successful deliverances is their propensity to sell or negotiate their prayers as a commodity. This type of job requires the exorcist to have a pure heart and remain humble.

Besides, the different types of deliverances depend on the degree of true faith the man of God actually has. It is crucial that he believes firmly that God will deliver the patient from whatever situation, because he is Almighty. Thus, when the faith of the man of God is not robust, when he is afraid or that he doubts his own ability, he cannot operate complicated deliverances such as the one of madness, blindness, epilepsy, HIV/AIDS, etc.

Finally, one should also understand that there are demons that can only go away through fasting and prayers. Thus, it is sometimes important to observe a period of fasting before proceeding to some types of deliverances. At times, one may fast for a week, two weeks, a month, or even several months when the case to be treated is complicated. During all that period, people concentrate in their church on imploring God's grace and action in the life of the victim. And when you get towards the end of the fasting period, the actual deliverance session can then start. Note that a deliverance session may start on a day and end on the following day. At times, the exorcist sweats a lot because it is a real battle. Certain demons leave the body while screaming like animals by shaking the victim; others merely leave without making any noise.

To corroborate this, I just want to give the example of a young man we recently received in our church of Obobogo (Yaounde) at the end of August 2009. His name is Paul Ndjambe. When he came, he was beset by madness crises. At that time, we were in the midst of a thirty-day program of evening prayers. This did not prevent us from starting another period of fasting in preparation for his deliverance. The spirit that inhabited him was ferocious and tough: the young boy manifested the energy of a buffalo. However, at the end of two weeks, he got successfully delivered. He is presently quiet and reasonable.

As you can understand from the above explanations, God does intervene in the life of human beings to deliver them from different inextricable situations. He uses his faithful servants to do so.

To come back to the experiences I have been learning from my sociolinguistics classes, I wish to point out that most of my students are Bamileke. This is an ethnic group that is very well known to be attached to its traditional practices. One such practice is the worship of the skull. From the point of view of Christianity, one would say that this practice is un-Christian. But this might be a wrong interpretation from some of us who are not Bamileke and who might not understand their culture more appropriately. Following their explanations, they say that their ancestors are a link between

God and them. That is, they still believe in the same almighty God that Christians believe in. The difference is that they consider their ancestors as being closer to God and therefore that they are the best intermediaries to help solve their problems as they are more likely to understand them. One of the counterarguments they usually give to Christians is: why do you have saints or the Virgin Mary in the Catholic religion? Isn't it because you believe that they are closer to God and that they can intervene for you when you invoke them? The concept of saints is western. It came with the imported religions. If Africans, and more particularly the Bamileke had been the most powerful community who had conquered Europe and imposed them their system of thinking, surely that the ancestors would have been accepted as the right intermediaries between God and human beings. For the Bamileke, they believe that they have so many testimonies that show that their ancestors do not belong to the realm of Satan. To them, God does use them to also help his children who have espoused the Christian religion. In the following testimony, a Bamileke girl recounts how her Christian faith and her belief in the power of her ancestors are not contradictory forces. On the contrary, they work in synergy to help them. Like the previous testimony, this one was originally written in French. The following is my translation of her text.

This testimony reveals a true story that took place in the town of Mbalmayo. My name is Decte Mevoutsa Doris Florine. I am a 27 year old student in linguistics, born in Mbalmayo. Both my parents are Bamileke and they are staunch believers, (more precisely Catholic practitioners). My parents just like other Bamileke people are very much influenced by their traditional culture. My story will show that, through the voice of the ancestors, our Lord God can convey a message and heed the prayer of his children, that is, us.

I originate from a dysfunctional family. My father and my mother are divorcees. My father has taken a second wife who is also from the west of Cameroon, that is, a Bamileke, from my father's own village. I live with my brother and sister in our family house. The re-marriage of my father was the beginning of our Calvary. His wife did not carry us in her heart. Our father no longer took care of us. He no longer inquired whether we had eaten or not, whether we were in good health or not, whether we went to school or not. One day, I fell ill. For a whole week, my brother told my father each morning that I was sick when he came by on his way to his work. As a response, he always answered that was not news at all and simply asked when I would recover. His wife behaved similarly. She was a housewife, which means that she stayed at home all day long. She always asked me when I would recover. For her, I was always sick, by all means.

On the seventh day of the week, I decided to leave my bed and confront my father to let him understand that I was seriously sick. By the time he was getting out to go to his job as he did every morning, I went towards him and while doing so, I collapsed in front of him. He gave 200 francs to my brother and asked him to bring me to my mother's place as my mother inhabited in the same town as ours. It was normally forbidden for us to visit my mother. After re-animating me with fresh water, my brother took me to my mother with great difficulty. When my mother saw me, she could not hold her tears. She started crying. She did not have any means to bring me to hospital. She then borrowed money from a woman's association (called tontine) and she thus brought me to the district hospital of the city where I stayed during one month and a half, hospitalized.

One morning, my maternal uncle called from the village to explain to my mother that there was an important ceremony in the village because of a strange phenomenon that took place there. In the Bamileke culture, there is what is called [syɛ]: the soil trembles in a particular place. This can be in a kitchen that has been abandoned by a grandmother, a mother, a father who is already dead, or in the playground of an abandoned concession. This phenomenon usually carries a message according to which a family member is seriously ill or is about to die. To avert this spell, people must perform a ceremony. That is why my uncle was inquiring about all the people to know whether there was someone who was sick. My mother responded that I was sick and that she was praying the Lord for my recovery.

The following evening my mother decided to bring me back home to let me breathe fresh air. After the meal, we sat down in order to pray as we did every evening. My mother was imploring the Lord so that he puts an end to my sickness of which no one really knew what caused it and how long it would last. For the medical doctors, I was suffering from amoebas. And yet, it was becoming very difficult for me to walk. At times, I was unable to recognize people, even my mother who, as time went on, intensified her prayers and supplications. While we were eating, someone knocked at the door. It was a stranger that we had never seen. Neither my mother, nor my brother, nor I had seen him before. He asked us if this was the house of a woman called Josephine. My mother did not answer. He then gave a set of indications that showed clearly that it was my mother that he was looking for.

He explained that he was coming from the village, and that he was a carrier of an important message. One ŋkamsyɛ (a traditional prophet) had sent him to look for someone who was very sick, who inhabits in this house and who runs the risk of dying if nothing is done. The lady prophet wanted us to bring this sick person to the village into her house. Note that this young messenger had never come to Mbalmayo and he did not even spend the night at our place. He simply gave us directions to get to the lady prophet and then went back after drinking some water.

The following morning, my mother went to borrow money from his "tontine," that is, from the woman's club. We then took the way to the village. When we got to the lady prophet, my mother and my sister were holding me to enable me to walk. When we wanted to cross the enclosure of her house, spasms ran through my body and I started screaming. My sister and my mother were obliged to put me on a makeshift bed on the road and then go and look for help from the lady prophet. She told them that she was waiting for them and that she had prepared a big can (bidon) of water of a doubtful color and salt. For three days, she made me drink that water. I was sleeping at her neighbor's until the fourth day when I was finally able to enter the prophet's house. Without telling me what I was suffering from, she took me with her to pluck leaves all night long with the use of a storm-lantern (lampe-tempête). My mother was asked to grind these leaves and mix them with soil, palm oil, salt, and a savage hen. That meal had to be my medication. During my stay at her place, the only medicine she gave me consisted of water, salt, and oil that she fetched from holes in her playground. She explained to my mother that the spirits are the ones who gave her directions as to which hole to fetch water from according to the case she was treating. At the end of our treatment, she asked for three savage hens that were very sturdy in order to remove from us the disease and the bad spirit. For my sister and my mother, the ritual only lasted two to three minutes. However, in my case, she put the hen on my head. I was kneeling down and the ritual lasted six hours to the extent that I was obliged to sit down on a stool because I was so tired. After six hours, the hen left my head which was weak and almost collapsing. The prophet said that it was crucial for the hen not to die, otherwise the spirits would again take possession of my body. She gave drinking water and corn to the hen which hesitated to eat. She succeeded nevertheless to compel it to drink the water. After about an hour, it started walking. At that moment, the disease left my body. One would have thought that I had never been sick as I was now able to walk without any help. This Nkamsyɛ did not ask money from my mother because, following what she said, she is not authorized to take money. What was even more curious is that she said that she did not know the young boy who made us come to the village.

That is how, thanks to the grace of God and through our ancestors' culture, I recovered from that disease of which the origin remains unknown to me up till now. Imagine that this young boy did not come to our place! My mother would never have the initiative of bringing me to the village. The first indication was the [syɛ]. I do not think that my mother would have gone there because she did not have money. She would have thought that it was not more important than her sick child. Thus the Lord used an intermediary person to give way to my recovery. I think that I will never thank him enough. This boils to one thing: the ways of the Lord are simply unfathomable. Amen!

This is really a fantastic story. I agree with the author who concludes that the ways of the Lord are unfathomable. She would have died if God did not use this traditional witch-doctor to treat her. And which kind of treatment! This was traditional treatment that most of us would not probably want to take if we were told that that is what we would be swallowing as medication. However, I think we should not construe God's intervention in this case as permission for Christians to consult soothsayers known as "marabouts" in Cameroon and in West Africa in general.

The following testimonies are by Yemeli Tiokeng Estelle. She is also a Bamileke girl. What is awe-inspiring from her testimonies is the experience she has personally had with evil spirits who came to visit her at night. Most non African people may not believe her story. But it is real. It is something that I have never personally experienced but I know of many people who have lived similar experiences. Imagine the fear that this creates in children. As recounted in her story, her absolute trust in God turned out to be the right weapon to fight these evil spirits.

As she writes, her testimony is about one of the most painful moments of her personal history, the death of her adoptive mother. Let us read her story (the original one is in French) from her own point of view.

My mother had diabetes during 20 years. Her illness worsened progressively, day in and day out, leading to complications such as hypertension of arteries and loss of sight. After several years of suffering, she finally passed away in March 2008, leaving us in atrocious suffering. My testimony deals with two aspects of God's power: his action through the neighbors and the way he dealt with the evil forces. I will then talk of the testimony of a friend of mine on the same issues.

It is generally accepted that God acts through his children, that is, human beings. I have experimented this precisely when my mother died.

First, the day of her burial, just after the burial, my brothers, my sister and some of my friends and I were in a taxi on our way back to the village of Mbouda. The car was driving at a high speed. That is when we saw women by the roads who were trying to stop the driver. The driver slowed down and succeeded to stop the car when he reached them. As soon as the car stopped, we got out of it and saw, with disgust and fright that the right hand back wheel was progressively separating from the car. This means that, without the help of these mothers who were coming from the field, we would have lost the wheel and capsized. I saw the hand of God who had just saved us from a terrible accident through these mothers.

That was not all. That same day, my younger brother made an accident on his motor cycle while coming to the mourning in the morning. Thus, as we arrived in Mbouda, I was ready to spend the night at the hospital. Through God's miracle, my younger brother got out merely with bruises on his nose, lacerations on his wrist, but no serious cerebral contusions. Thanks to God's intervention, our aunt from my mother's side was able to convince the hospital authorities to give us a loan for the hospitalization of my younger brother. I say this because my father did not have a single cent on him, and we too were absolutely penniless. We thus found ourselves with a loan for 80 thousand CFA francs that we had to reimburse before we would be allowed to leave the hospital.

Again, I was able to spot God's miracle. Despite the expenses and the problems we had in the family as a consequence of the mourning, we were able to collect from all the members of the family 80 thousand francs in less than two days. It was just a desperate situation for which a solution was found in no time. Glory be to God!

Now that my brother had left the hospital, I was persuaded that my problems were over. This turned out to be wrong. The evil spirits were ready to play dirty tricks on me. The whole phenomenon started with the presence of an owl on top of our gate during the night. In our customs, sighting an owl in such circumstances is an indication of the presence of vampires. About one week later, I got my first experience with evil forces. I was in my room reading a novel. It was around 1 AM, that is, an hour after midnight, when I heard birds flying; this was followed by the screaming of the owl at my window. I got the impression that the air had suddenly got electrified with evil substance and I got so frightened that my body began to shiver. I was so frightened that my first reaction was to cover my head with the blanket. Soon after this, I came to my senses. I then looked for my booklet of prayers that I always had at my bedside since the day of the funeral. After finding it, I took some anointed water that I kept in my room and poured it around the window. I also scattered blessed salt in my room and around that window as well. The screams of the owl stopped for a while, but they started all over again a few minutes later. I then started to recite the circumstantial prayers which were in my prayer booklet. When I finished reciting those prayers, I started singing because I belong to a choir. I thus sang until five o'clock in the morning. It is then that I realized that the air had become serene again and that the screams of the owl had completely stopped. Nonetheless, I continued to sing until five thirty. I then slept soundly after giving thanks to God for his help that he had just provided me in these difficult times.

This experience affected me a great deal because I realized that we were now exposed to evil forces with no protection from our deceased mother who used to pray a lot for us when she was alive. That terrible experience was not going to be the last, unfortunately.

On the eve of my trip from Mbouda, I had another experience that was even worse. That night, I arranged my luggage until around midnight and a half. After that, I took a novel and read it as usual. Curiously enough, I began dosing. In my half sleep, I heard once more the owl howling on my window. I stood up in this semi-conscious state in order to pour anointed water on the window, and then I went back to sleep. Then, as if I was half dreaming, I saw the owl going around the house and coming to stop in front of the door, infiltrate itself through the underside of the door, multiply itself, and start making a lot of noise in the living room. This time, as I became frightened, I just woke up. Curiously enough, the noise I heard in my dream was real. I thought at that moment that my younger brother had risen to study. At the same time, I pushed away that idea, telling myself that he could not make such awful noise at night. I then became really frightened and felt as if I was paralyzed. I became unable to even recite a prayer to chase away these evil spirits. However, with God's grace, I succeeded to come back to my senses and to recite prayers of deliverance along with religious songs. I prayed and sang so much that, at the end of almost two hours and a half, the noise stopped abruptly. I continued to sing for a while before I mustered enough courage to get out of my room. I saw that the living room was empty and that there was no single book of my brother on the table. This confirmed that he did not get up during the night. I felt so fortunate for that because I would not want to guess what would have then happened.

As soon as it became daylight, my younger brothers accompanied me to the bus station for my trip back to Yaounde. As I left home, my heart was at pains because I was very worried. I was wondering under whose protection I was leaving my younger brothers with. The answer came as a flash: God. Twice, he had helped me get rid of the evil spirits from the house, and he is the one who has always taken care of us.

These testimonies on the presence of God in my life are merely a few among many others. This does not only occur to me. I would like to recount a testimony from a very close friend of mine. Upon her elder sister's death, her family had to face evil spirits that were fierce. These spirits had taken hold of the house. They used to walk on the roof and even in the corridors of the house, compelling all the family to take refuge in their mother's bedroom. The family decided to organize prayer sessions called "neuvaines" in French and also to recite Hail Mary's as often as they could. They prayed for a long time until the faces of those who were threatening them through those evil spirits were revealed to them. Since that moment, the neighbors began to detest these evil people by calling them witches. With the prayers that continued, some of the neighbors left the quarter. After that, the bad spirits stopped wandering around the house and the family has thus regained peace again.

From my own experience, I strongly believe in the existence of God and that he still operates miracles in our daily lives. This is why the demon seeks to counteract his actions and is always on the lookout to tempt us when we feel most vulnerable, for example, during the mourning period. The work of the devil is always to spoil, to destroy what God has built and arranged. God certainly loves us and is kind towards us. He simply requires us to pray him with fervor and faith in order for him to heed our prayers, mostly in difficult times. He is omnipotent and he can do anything. He wants us to trust him so that he may accomplish miracles in every domain of our lives. What I am today, I solely owe it to the Lord my savior who is God the Father, the Son, and the Holy Spirit. That is why I say to him with my deepest sincere feelings: Glory and praise to you, oh Lord!

The next set of stories is from a woman who is special to me in that I consider her as rather mysterious. I had known her some seven years earlier. She then disappeared completely from my life. I never understood why. She is this student I became friends with at a time I was collecting information about an AIDS prevention book I was planning to write. When I became close to her, I thought she would be a key student to help spread the message of AIDS prevention among the university community. She was a cheerleader at the University of Yaounde. Through my interactions, I noticed that she was friends with influential political authorities. However, I was never sure of her commitment. In my mind, I thought that she was this typical Cameroonian girl who would readily accept different partners as long as they provide her with amenities that the so-called sugar daddies give to university girls. She thus represented the girls who were at high risk with respect to the AIDS virus. I was probably wrong. Seven years later, I saw her in my office. At first, I could not recognize her immediately. But I did, although I had forgotten her name completely. She told me that she was going to become my student and that I was one of two teachers with whom she wanted to renew contact to encourage her to do linguistics. She was so enthusiastic that I was very happy to see her. I must also confess that, in our subsequent interactions, I still found her extremely mysterious. She was very open with me, at the same time, I noticed that she did not accept that I have close relationships with other girls who are her classmates. She simply could not accept such an idea and she was adamant about that. To me, I thought that she would simply be my friend. One day, she revealed me part of her personal identity, notably that she was a married woman with three children. She also explained to me that she also lost one of her children a few years back. One day, she met me on campus and told me that she had learned about the death of my daughter Georgina. She presented her condolences. I could see that she was a very caring mother and that she fully understood how difficult it is for a parent to lose his child. Since she was one of my sociolinguistics students who got the assignment of writing a paper about God's intervention in preparation for the book I planned to write for Georgina's recovery, she told me that she had already written down her testimonies and that she would bring them on the following day. Before you start reading them, I just want to say that one should never judge other people's behavior on the basis of mere appearances. Although I always considered this student mysterious, sometimes, in the negative sense, her testimonies reveal that she has this "divine bud" in her that probably guides her life and protect her and her family, and that, through these stories, she can further convey this divine bud message to our readers so that we may accept God's empowerment in our lives to contribute to the fulfillment of this divine wish, "thy will be done on earth as it is in heaven." The following are her stories (originally written in French).

"Stories of God's intervention in man's life" by N.A.Y.

In 1999, in the city of Bafia, a young boy who was enrolled as a student in a secondary school saw the power of God manifest itself in his life. In fact, as he came from a neighboring village to pursue his studies, he was frequently the target of open oral attacks from his paternal uncles who did not want him to go to school. Their own children had abandoned their studies very early on, some of them had become jobless and alcoholic, and others had become simple farmers. Those uncles could not stand seeing this young boy pursue his studies. At various occasions, these witches had cast spells on him as well as mystical diseases; at times he nearly died because they had bewitched him. Fortunately, he always succeeded to survive because of the prayers that his poor mother always addressed to God for his protection. Every time she went to church to pray, she crossed over the playground of one of these witches who constantly told her that, soon or later, they would kill that child and that her "small prayers" would prove irrelevant. But the boy's mother never listened to him. She persevered in her prayers.

When he reached the age of 16, that is, when he was in the fourth form of secondary school, his parents decided to take him away from these evil people by sending him to Bafia for his studies. His mother recommended him to never give up praying. He was to always go to church on Sunday and he was to always praise and pray his God as soon as he wakes up and when he goes to bed at night. However, he sort of became blinded by the activities of the city; playing games with his comrades was his favorite pastime, and he somehow thus neglected his prayers. He usually woke up and slept without even thinking of addressing a single prayer to God. As the "enemy never sleeps," his detractors kept on playing dirty tricks on him by visiting him, mystically, at night.

One afternoon, the young boy went with his friends to the stadium to watch a football match. On his way back, he found that his small room made of planks and that he was renting at "Rymis" neighborhood got completely consumed by fire. Everything was burnt to ashes and apparently nothing had been salvaged from the fire. No one really understood where the fire came from and why it even happened at all. However, the boy was to witness a spectacular vision: although everything had burnt, only the little table at his bedside on which his Bible laid and that he had not even opened for several weeks was still intact. Yes, the Bible had not been touched by the flames. This was really unbelievable but true. An arson that had ravaged everything had been unable to even touch the small table, let alone the Bible. The neighbors who precipitated themselves to extinguish the fire had been unable to master it. Everybody was surprised to see the small table and the Bible spared by the fire. From that moment, the boy understood that God's power was within his Word written down in the Bible. That is why this mystical fire had been unable to reach the Word of God. As he was still distressed, he went to his village and recounted the sad story to his mother. All the family assembled and started to pray hard for a period of nine days and fasted for three days asking God to avenge their son. To them, the culprits of this arson were to be punished. They kept asking Almighty God to heed their prayers. The fourth day, they saw two uncles coming to kneel down before the parents of the young boy to confess their evil and implore their forgiveness. They said that they felt something like the fire of the Holy Spirit constantly burning them. The mother of the young boy advised them to repent and to give their lives completely to Christ. However, they categorically refused. That same night, these two uncles died inside their houses after a sudden short illness.

One can see from this testimony that God of the poor, God of the just, God of the miserable had acted in the life of the young boy by proving to him his fidelity, power and force through the destruction of his enemies. Years later, the young boy succeeded to obtain his diploma and for the time being he is an employee at the ministry of primary education. He still worships God who has operated miracles in his life.

Two months ago, at Emombo quarter, more precisely, at a place called Belibi junction, a horrible scene was about to take place if God had not intervened. There was this man who had kidnapped a little child and hid her for ten days. The man was a rich man whose strange business turned out to be dealing in child trafficking. Guess what! This was a nine-year old child who was the unique girl in a family with five boys.

As the girl came back from the grocery store of the quarter, she was kidnapped by that trafficker and was then locked in an underground room of a tall building this trafficker owned. He possessed an enormous snake which used to swallow the children and then spat out bank notes. That is what explained this trafficker's pseudo wealth. The girl's family was extremely pious. After looking for their child for a long time, they realized that she had simply disappeared. They immediately started praying intensely, imploring everyday the Lord to bring back their child, safe and sane.

As for the little girl, the only prayer that she knew was"

Our father who art in heaven
Hallowed be thy name
Thy kingdom come
Thy will be done on earth as it is in heaven
Give us this day our daily bread
And forgive us our trespasses
As we forgive those who trespass against us
And lead us not into temptation
But deliver us from evil
For the kingdom, the power and the glory are yours
Now and for ever
Amen.

Every evening, she would recite her prayer and sleep on a piece of cardboard that the kidnapper had given her as her bed. Late at night, she would see in the dim light a gigantic snake that came towards her to devour her. The first evening, she got so panicked that she fainted before the terrific beast. Nevertheless, she found herself unexpectedly safe and sane in the morning when she woke up. She then recalled the recommendations from her mother who kept telling her and her five brothers that one should never give up, whatever obstacle one faces, since nothing is impossible to God. He is the almighty. So, whenever it became night time, she always succeeded to overcome her fear and kept reciting her prayer. The monster would come, turn around her several times and then go away through the same way it came. The kidnapper could not understand why his totem was unable to swallow that child. He waited some more time. On the other side, the girl's elder brother had a vision that revealed to him that his young sister was still alive and that it was necessary to pray even harder so that she might be freed. He revealed his dream to his mother and all of them prayed and made offers and holocausts to the Lord.

On the ninth day, the kidnapper's wife who ignored all the devilish activities of her spouse discovered the little girl locked in the dark underground, as she was going to park old furniture that she had decided to get rid of that day (yes, precisely that day). She talked to the child and decided to free her right away; she felt enough energy in herself to counteract her husband's wrath. That is how the little girl had her life saved thanks to the intervention of the Most High who manifested his power in the family of this little girl, through the little girl herself, and mostly through the wife of the kidnapper as he used her to free the little girl.

Cameroon is a country of all sorts of freedoms. With the liberalization of the religious sector, several new churches, called revival churches, have sprouted. Most of the times, these churches are headed by pastors who do their best not only to try to get a multitude of followers, but also to accomplish "miracles" in the name of Jesus. They thus succeed to win the unbelievers' hearts and the most vulnerable people in a bid to extort big amounts of money from them and to impoverish them further.

In one of these new revival churches, one of the gurus who worked under the empowerment of a voodoo had become an expert in making miracles. He used to have a special insignia in the form of a horse on his left hand small finger, which is the sign of his alliance with Satan. Moreover, he used a special perfume and a crucifix that he used to make the people he touched to faint. One day, he entered his secret room to get ready for the celebration of a church service. This would be a special church service because, among the congregation, there was a rich business man who had health problems. He was told that he had come there because he was possessed by evil spirits and that he needed to attend a deliverance special session. That is why he came to that church in order to regain peace and hopefully total recovery. The false pastor immediately sensed that he was going to make money and that he needed to make the best performance of his career by extirpating the devils from the body of this rich business man. He knew that, at the end of a successful performance, he would receive a huge gift. He thus entered his room, but, curiously enough, he did not find his crucifix and his perfume. He went out of the room very disconcerted. The time of the celebration of the church service was overdue. The congregation was waiting for him. When he went back into his secret room for the second time, a big light blinded him and he fell down with his face on the floor. He then sensed the presence of Jesus Christ in front of him who spoke to him thus: "You have been using my name for your devilish jobs; since now on, you will be serving me for real. You will have to repent in front of the congregation, reveal them all your misdeeds and present to them your "work tools," that is, your ring, the crucifix, and the perfume. After you have done that, I will give you power, the real power, the power that comes from my father. But you will not be taking money because the word of God is not a commodity for sale.

The pastor did exactly what the Lord asked him to do and he became invested with power that was far above the one he had received from the voodoo. It was no longer necessary for him to knock down his followers to deliver them from evil spirits, or to make them faint as he used to do in the past. He simply needed to pray to operate miracles without any special agitations. He got a special ointment to make people recover. He could tell a blind person "open your eyes and see!" The miracle would be accomplished. He thus fulfilled his mission from that day on, with the strict prohibition of accepting money or gifts.

As I was just finishing reading these stories, another student of mine, Linda Amang, popped into my office. She told me that she also had a testimony she wanted to give me. This testimony was about Prophet T.B. Joshua.

I was a bit reluctant to include testimonies from the TV in a book like this. It is true that these TV testimonies are absolutely astounding. But, as we get used to them, one wonders if they are not made up. Are they really genuine? I know that they are. Otherwise, people would not be coming from all over the world to Nigeria to obtain deliverance from Prophet Joshua. I believe, from a scientific point of view, as long as we do not have an alternative explanation for the deliverance events and miracles that are aired on this Nigerian TV of Prophet Joshua, we have to accept them, maybe with a pinch of salt. I do not know how the various official churches view these miracles. I think about the Catholics because Prophet Joshua must be Protestant. I also think about Christian denominations, as well as other religions like Islam. Do they accept them as coming from God?

Again, if each of us can look inside himself, without the pressure of the outside world, he will find that there is something genuine in these deliverances and miracles. They are certainly likely to stir up the divine bud that exists in all of us, no matter which religion we belong to, and remind us that there is a God who can intervene in our lives and answer our prayers. Even if he does not answer these prayers, at least we must know that, somewhere, upon our death, we will certainly meet him and account for our deeds here on earth. I believe the great majority of people do not need these miracles in order to believe in God. Most people do live a normal life and they do believe that they are the artisans of their own future life. For some people, being an artisan of one's future does not necessarily imply that God has to be involved.

Yet, if you think about certain natural catastrophes that have been wrecking the world, you cannot be sure that your life is secure one hundred percent. Think about the inhabitants of the island of Sumatra in Indonesia and those of Thailand who were the victims of a deadly Tsunami that instantly killed more than 320 thousand people in sixteen countries of south-east Asia. Think about the people of the city of New Orleans in the States who faced the ill consequences of the Katrina cyclone that destroyed their houses. Think about the victims in the rain that has recently destroyed properties in Turkey. As was announced on the radio this morning (September 10, 2009), within 4 hours, the equivalent of rain that had fallen for six years fell in Turkey and it engulfed cars that were in the streets and flooded houses and so on. Think of the earthquakes that have leveled many houses in various countries such as Turkey, China, Mexico, etc. Even if you are very careful about your life, know that you could have been at a particular spot and be swept away by such catastrophes and eventually die. Unfortunately, this will still not prevent you from accounting for your life on earth before the divine judge. What these natural catastrophes should tell us is that our daily survival on this planet Earth remains a miracle as well and that we owe this miracle to this Supreme Being who, at any time, may decide to call us back to him. That is why, we'd better always remain prepared to meet him and take this personal decision of amending our own lives so as we may be artisans in building a world where the slogan of this book is accomplished, notably, "thy will be done on earth as it is in heaven."

I am now going to let you read Linda Amang's testimony about Prophet Joshua. You will discover that it is amazing in that, if you really have deep faith in God, you may benefit from Joshua's miracles even at your own place through the TV program, by means of the very screen of your TV.

The following is the text Linda Amang submitted as her testimony of God's intervention through Prophet Joshua.

Not long ago, I returned from school and I met my mum crying and explaining something to my dad. My mum's disposition really affected me that I had to go and ask her what the problem was. This is what she told me. She said that in the afternoon, when she was watching television, precisely "Emmanuel RV" (a channel on TV that always shows how a recent prophet in Nigeria, Prophet T.B. Joshua of the synagogue Church of All Nations, who heads and delivers people from all sorts of bondage) the prophet was giving a healing session. He was asking all viewers and those present in church at that moment to meditate on all the obstacles they have been having in their lives. Particularly to the viewers the prophet asked them to move towards their screens and touch them. My mum says, while meditating on her own personal problems, she moved towards the TV screen.

Mum has been having problems with her sight for the past twenty years. She cannot read or write without lenses. She says that immediately after she touched the TV screen, the prophet started saying prayers of deliverance and she too was praying and asking God to help deliver her from her sight problems with the belief that God was going to answer her prayers. After a few minutes of prayers (while still having her hand on the TV screen), mum says she felt so strange and it was as if something she cannot explain was leaving her body. It was like her eyes got dark, and tears started flowing from them. Mum says she started shouting out in joy as she could no longer feel the usual pain she used to feel in her eyes.

Immediately, she noticed the writings on the screen which she always finds difficult to read, were so easily read by her eyes. She also moved into her room, picked up a book and discovered that she could easily read this book without any strain or lenses. Later on the day when my elder sister returned home, mum told her what had happened, but my elder sister laughed and told mum not to bother her with such a fake story. This is what sent mum into tears and when dad returned from work she was then explaining it to him.

Of late, mum no longer wears her lenses and she tells us that she faces no problem without them. She can read, write, move under the hot sun without her lenses.

Mum received this healing because she believed that God could do it for her. She is not the only individual who follows T.B. Joshua's sermons and healing sessions. Many do. But the question is: do they watch it like any other channel to be entertained or they watch it because they believe that through the channel they could be saved and healed from their troubles? This is where the problem lies. God can only manifest in the lives of those who believe in his existence. If we do not believe that something exists, then how can we expect that thing to manifest in our lives? I think that testimonies like these should leave skeptics with no options but an acceptance of God's powers and supremacy. We should note that there is nothing like a European or foreign God. There is only one God who takes care of everyone irrespective of the social condition or race. If he really is a God of the white man, how come he could heal my mum? Is my mum white? She definitely is not.

A few personal comments are in order here. I saw deliverance sessions on TV that Prophet Joshua led in Korea and Australia. They cannot be fake sessions. At the same time, they show that this phenomenon of spirit possession is universal; it is not something that only happens to black people. Even during the Nigerian deliverance sessions, white people are among the audience and they undergo the agitations just like other people. I do not know which argument one could give to deny these facts. God exists and, as I know it, he will ask us to account for our actions upon our death. So, we'd better contribute to establishing his kingdom here on earth by acting in such a way that his will be done on earth as it is in heaven.

The following testimony is a further appeal to always be on our guards in our daily dealings. It is particularly relevant in African societies where, from what I have been learning from my sociolinguistics students, there are people who are tempted to obtain money from the devil. This is something that has always been very difficult for me to understand. But many Cameroonians certainly understand it because such events seem to be common in their society. I am also convinced that similar events take place in other parts of the African continent. Certainly, they do happen in my own native country, the DRC, because I have learned that, in the 1970's, some tradesmen in my area used to deal with the sale of human heads. It seems that they usually targeted heads that have a few grey hairs as these were on high demand for making magic. I do not personally know any person who got killed because of this, but this does not mean that people were not killed. As you read this following testimony, the message you will certainly get is that it is a testimony that is an illustration of what happens when you make a pact with the devil. The devil is primarily a liar, and he makes you do horrible things. The ultimate message is to avoid any temptation of easy money through devilish acts. Soon or later, that same devil will turn against you unless you give your life to God.

A testimony from Cecilia Njolle about secret dealings with the devil.

Before I start this testimony, a word about a disease called aneurism is in order here as it will intervene in the text I am going to recount.

Aneurism is a localized widening (dilation) of an artery, vein or the heart. At the area of aneurysm, there is typically a bulge and the wall is weakened and may rupture. Brain aneurism is a small aneurism that looks like a berry; it ruptures frequently and bleeds.

Mr. Makongo was the father of two with no health problems, when all of a sudden he felt a terrible headache.

124

Before that, Mr. Makongo lived a very rough life: playboy, cheating on his wife, smoking, drinking up to the point that he was being initiated by a friend in a secret society without his knowing. His friend just told him to attend a meeting of important people of the region. The meeting had to take place at 11 PM. He did not ask what they were doing there. He thought his friend was entirely trustworthy, so he took his car and went to the meeting. When he arrived there he was welcomed by the other men who wore red suits, which was strange. After the discussion, information, and the rest, they asked the cook to set the table. The cook just brought a big bowl covered with a white veil. After that, they announced the arrival of the "boss" of their cult. He wore black and had red eyes. Mr. Makongo started having goose pimples and asked his friend the permission to go home. His friend told him he cannot go because if he does, he will go and tell the others what they are doing. The big boss hypnotized him and asked his friend if he is the person to initiate. His friend said yes. The big boss asked him to go to the table to drink and eat. Before the table, he saw blood in a cup and when they opened the bowl of food, he saw a baby. The boss asked him to serve himself. He shouted and refused but the big boss hypnotized him and made him burst the child's eyes and cut his ears. Mr. Makongo heard the painful voice of the baby crying, shouting, moaning and dying of pain. Having drunk the cup of blood, he told him to go back home and that he will see his room full of money. Mr. Makongo could not believe it. His friend looked at him from afar and laughed. For him, he thought he was in a dream but it was the reality. The big boss told him that if he tells what happened at that meeting, he will curse him by sending him an illness and he will die. That day, Mr. Makongo was calm and this was unusual. His wife came to ask if anything was the matter. He merely looked at her but couldn't say anything. He entered his room and saw money everywhere inside it. He shouted as he got utterly frightened. His wife came, saw the money and collapsed. She woke up ten minutes later and asked the whereabouts of that money that he did not inform her about in advance. His wife was so inquisitive that Mr. Makongo finally told her what happened and informed her that he will die after what he has revealed to her. The immediate reaction of his wife, as a Christian, was to go and see a pastor and expose him the problem. The pastor told Mrs. Makongo to come the next day with her husband. That very next day, Mr. Makongo felt a terrible headache. Within a few minutes, he felt himself collapsing onto the floor like a bag of potatoes and his last thought was that it has happened, he will die. A short time later his first daughter Mary, who was the oldest of his children, came in the house, found him, and took him to the hospital.

At the hospital, they had no clue as to what was wrong until they ruled out a heart attack and they realized that it must be the head. He had a big cerebral bleed. An all day operation was called for but even then death was very likely. His wife was a strong Christian and she asked individuals and the whole church to pray for him in the name of Jesus Christ. During the operation, Mr. Makongo who was in a coma saw a white light from afar coming near. He saw the hand of somebody carrying and pulling him on crumbs of bottles. While pulling, the person said he is doing this to remove the blood he drank. Mr. Makongo shouted because it was painful and he had wounds all over his body. Before going, the man said: "you are my child and as you go, live a better life." He then put his hand on his forehead and went. His hand was soft and fresh and the man disappeared.

After the operation the doctors told his wife he will either die or be brain dead. Two days after, the doctors did some analysis and saw nothing of the kind; meanwhile they wanted to see if they could mend his brain. It was surprising to observe that a man who went through surgery and whose situation was near death could thus be back to normal two days after. Unbelievable! When he woke up, he told his wife what happened and his wife told him it was God's intervention. Mr. Makongo lives a Christian life and heard that his friend who initiated him died by a car accident.

Chapter 8

Living With the Divine Bud

What if Georgina is really a saint! I know, from the official point of view of the Catholic religion, this may not be the case because the Pope has neither canonized her nor proclaimed her a saint. But you and I know pretty well that there are millions of saints unknown to the Pope. We also know that God, in his sovereignty, knows who is a saint and who is not. We too may have the feeling that someone has become a saint because we believe that he has been a true disciple of God here on earth. I certainly know one woman from my village in eastern DRC, more precisely, in the village of Kitsuku in Northern Kivu, who has led the life of a saint. I would say that she was the equivalent of Mother Theresa of Calcutta. Her name is Magdalene. Her life was truly an instantiation of what the Lord wants people to do in terms of loving the destitute. In our village, she was always ready to give a helping hand to such destitute, with an open heart. She never showed any revulsion towards them. Now that she is dead and that the official clergy in the area could never afford presenting her case even to the local church in order to canonize her, she will never be proclaimed as a saint. No one will ever know about her deeds that would qualify her as a saint.

Even as we speak about official sainthood, I personally believe that there is a lot of injustice in the whole enterprise of proclaiming certain people saints by the Pope. There are a lot of administrative procedures involved, and certainly a lot of money. You have to belong to a community of rich people to be proclaimed a saint. This may not be true, but imagine that a dossier has to be constituted. There must be official representatives of the Pope who would check on the deeds of that person. A lot of expenses are usually involved and this can only be done if the family or maybe the parish can afford such expenses. As one thinks about it, it is not surprising that most saints on the Catholic calendar will be from Europe, mostly from Italy and France. Does this mean that, in the whole world, it is mostly the French and the Italians who are saints? This cannot be true. Saints are everywhere and only God knows who they are because they are his friends in heaven. To such saints unknown here on earth, we do assure you that we also admire you. The one day that has been proclaimed as Saints' day by the Catholic religion is in remembrance of you. We nonetheless pray that you constantly look after us, that you also intervene for us so that most of us, still living, be able to join you upon our death and that, we succeed to change our behavior in a way that, every one of us in whatever position we occupy, we work towards the accomplishment of the words in the Lord's prayer, notably, "thy will be done on earth as it is in heaven." We pray that you join us in praying God to particularly heed our prayers for all our human projects that seek to make people accept him as the ultimate authority in our personal lives and that his Holy Spirit be the one that inspires us into doing the right things for ourselves and for our neighbors. As saints, you certainly know what is right for us and what is likely to further render the name of God "hallowed." I truly wish that if you do have that power of intervening for us, please do that. God is more likely to heed our prayers if you help us pray him in the way he wants to be prayed so that he may accede to our requests that are likely to further contribute to the arrival of his kingdom on earth and to true peace, justice, and love that would grow as the logical consequence of doing "thy will as is done in heaven."

In the case of Georgina, to me and also to all those people who have given us testimonies about her, she is certainly a saint. She is the epitome of the divine bud in that she was not sullied at all. Before elaborating on this notion of "divine bud" in a way that it would benefit the humanity who hopefully will read this book, I would like to give further information about Georgina. After all, if she were recognized as a saint by the official Catholic Church, people would want to know every detail about her. I do not think we need to know such details. At the same time, the information I will now give about her is merely to make us picture what a sixteen year old child, who did not know that she would be a saint, before she went to Ghana, left as immediate memories upon her death. This is a girl who, when she went to Ghana, she was convinced that God was going to use Dr. Boachie to give her a corrected body. What happened, God rather called her back to him, making sure that her body would remain unscarred by any surgical operation.

First, here is another excerpt of the obituary notes I wrote about her. It concerns my own testimony as her father.

As my preparation for her coming back from Ghana, I wished that we be able to show to the world that the Lord God has heeded our prayers by allowing this surgical operation. Before they traveled to Ghana, Georgina, her younger sister Nadine, and her mother Jacky addressed each a thanksgiving prayer that showed how God was attentive to our prayers. As for me, I was preparing myself, in secret, with my students of Masters I and II in sociolinguistics at the University of Yaounde 1, to provide me with testimonies that

131

show how God acts in our lives. I wanted, subsequently, to write a book from these testimonies that would invite men and women to accept God in our lives so that he be inspiring our actions and our behavior. The book was to be entitled "Divine Bud" and I wanted this book to be written in the spirit of realizing the statements in the prayer that we learned from the Lord, notably, "thy will be done on earth as it is in heaven." I wanted to tell people that, despite the pains that we experiment, we should never get discouraged. God is attentive to our prayers.

As for us, people would certainly be tempted to say that God did not heed our prayer because Georgina is dead. This is not true. God is God. He knows us more than we know ourselves. He is that one who decided to call Georgina back to Him. We harbor very good memories of Georgina. I was deeply touched by messages of compassion that came in great numbers from several people in order to support us morally. What I presently ask you is, if you ever have a personal message or you know a message from one of your friends that you know that God intervened in his life, please communicate it to us. Maybe, we could publish it in a book. I have already got some from the University of Yaounde 1. My email address is: pmutaka@gmail.com.

In what follows, please read the testimonies of four people: two Protestant Christians, (one is Cameroonian and the other American), one Catholic from the DRC, and one Buddhist from Germany. The first one was written in French.

My dear brother Mutaka,

As I am writing this note, I really have a great quantity of tears flowing from my eyes. Mary had just announced this bad news to me while crying. She was unable to reach the end of her news. Yes, she has gone to heaven to her father who wanted to spare her the sufferings of the planet Earth. We would have preferred that she remains in our midst in her state. Man proposes but God takes the ultimate decision. What you have done, you did it out of sheer love that parents have for their children. You did your duty, you do not have to worry about that. Be courageous, we are with you in this pain; your suffering is also ours. May the soil of our ancestors be light to her and that the Lord our God welcome her in heaven. We pray this with our utmost faith.

Courage! my dear brother.

Nduire Kakungu Cardinal.

Dear Philip,

I have just received this message of the passing away into eternity of Georgina! You did tell me Jacky was taking her to Ghana for the operation and we were hoping for the best. It is upsetting, but God's will is supreme. It is gratifying to hear the testimony of her faith in the Lord. It is nevertheless a painful loss. Lucy joins me in sending you and Jacky our heartfelt condolences. Our prayer is that the Lord will strengthen you in times like these.

Sammy Chumbow

Let me just insert another message of Professor Chumbow here that he sent me as his reaction to the reading of the Divine bud manuscript. My wish is that you also check the passage he mentions in Deuteronomy 30: 15, 19. It is so true.

Dear Philip,

Your testimony of Georgina's prayer the night before her departure to Ghana, coming after Jacky's, and her letter to her siblings, Nadine and Eric, on the eve of her departure through the pearly gates of splendor to be with the Lord, is very touching. It reminds me of our own son, Nde Chumbow who at the age of eight, was called to be with the Lord after only an unusually very brief illness! Neurologists had declared at three years, that he had the brain tracings of an adult and at five he was very popular in school for his crusade to protect weak children from bullies. No one young or old who met him was left indifferent. And then suddenly he left like a meteor when everyone expected him to grow up into a genius. The reason I am sharing this with you is that, after Nde's departure, Rev. Professor Michael Bame Bame, former Dean of the Faculty of Protestant Theology here in Yaounde and author of the book 'Death and Everlasting life', told us emphatically that children like Nde whom he knew well (and I believe Georgine too) are special gifts from God to humanity with a special mission warrant and are recalled as soon as the mission is completed. The Bame's were blessed with one such child whose presence and intervention in their home they still feel from time to time. Rev. Bame Bame is one whose experiential knowledge of God is profound and who has been used by God to bless many in terms of divine healing of the type in the testimonies of some of our students. Let Nadine and Eric know that when Georgine says she will be "watching," it is not a joke, it is divine prophecy! She is seated on the highest pinnacle of heavenly glory among what St Paul calls a "crowd of witnesses" cheering their every victorious move and interceding as need arises.

134

The testimonies from our students are believable from my own knowledge of similar situations. Some underscore the existence of evil and its champion the devil. Others underscore the power of God, the author of life and Goodness whose power overcomes evil and the darkness of this world and the world to come.

There are two antagonistic forces daily contending for our attention and adherence: the forces of goodness and the forces of evil. Adherence to the forces of evil means curses and death and a choice of the forces of goodness means blessings and life everlasting. That is why the Bible tells us in Deuteronomy 30:15 to19 to choose the way that leads to life.

I believe your book will have a lasting impact on all who read it and to God be the Glory.

Sammy Chumbow

Dear Philip,

I'm so sorry that Georgina's operation did not result in her recovery, but in her death. My wife and I will be praying for you during the days and weeks ahead as you grieve and adjust to this huge loss. May the peace of God be your experience each day during this difficult time and may the Holy Spirit himself comfort each member of your family.

Your colleague and friend,

Steve

Dearest Philip,

Your news came as quite a shock to me; I can only try to imagine how much more of a shock it was to you and Jacky and to Nadine and Eric.

Please accept my most heartfelt sympathies for the loss of your beloved little daughter. I am so grateful that I have had the chance to meet her, even if only briefly. Such a joyful, beautiful and courageous little girl! Georgina will live on in the hearts of everyone who knew her, I am sure.

I am also deeply touched by your strong faith. You might know that I myself am not a Christian, I am a Buddhist. If I may, I would like to offer a little consolation from the Buddhist perspective. I hope it will not offend your own feelings; it is just my way of sharing my feelings with you.

Buddhism views life as eternal. One could liken it to the ocean. Each individual is a wave at once its own and always connected to the whole. As the wave breaks over the water to re-merge with it - this is death. As with the ocean this wave will emerge again in another form at another time and place. As a result we always remain connected.

Georgina's life was like a majestic crowning wave breaking on the water, causing all who knew her to feel that life is indeed beautiful and can be lived with joy and courage under all circumstances. Please know that as we are all waves in this big ocean my prayers always reach you - AND Georgina - wherever you are. I believe we can support each other with prayer and I believe distance does not matter as we are all connected at the heart level.

My heart is with you all!!

Love from your friend Britta

I wish the author of this last message to know that I greatly appreciated it. As I found it very much philosophical, I decided to share it with an American professor, Pat Schneider that I mentioned earlier, so that she might also appreciate it. I just want to emphasize this utterance in the message: *"Georgina's life was like a majestic crowning wave breaking on the water, causing all who knew her to feel that life is indeed beautiful and can be lived with joy and courage under all circumstances."* This is a message which, if shared by everybody who will read this book, will hopefully make people view life from a more positive perspective. In a sense, it encapsulates the central message of this book in that it seeks to present Georgina's early demise as part of the divine bud that would contribute to make these words of our Lord "thy will be done on earth as it is in heaven" become reality. I am convinced that, if we put these words in practice, we will be able to feel that life is indeed beautiful and can be lived with joy and courage under all circumstances.

Speaking of Pat Schneider, she recently sent me an email message in which she declared that Georgina's life had also truly impacted her although she had never seen her. She wrote me that it would be an absolute honor for her to proofread this novel we were writing on behalf of Georgina. Most importantly, she specifically wrote, "see how many people all over the world she has touched [...] (Georgine is a very beautiful name by the way-- it is originally from Greek (Georgia) and it means of the Earth, farmer. St. George is the patron saint of Greece). Several years ago I wrote to the nun whom I met when she visited our church and she was telling of a great miracle she experienced (read this: http://silouanthompson.net/2009/04/interview-sister-aemiliane/.You can see that she was crushed under those collapsed bridges. The crushing was in such a way that it reminded me of the suffering Georgine experienced from the curvature of her back crushing her lungs. So I wrote to Sister Aemiliane and asked her to pray for Georgine, which she did and I wrote her again more recently to ask her to pray for her after Georgine died and to pray for your whole family." Don't you find this message reassuring and confirming my hope that telling Georgina's story might truly impact the world? My readers should perhaps be informed that Pat belongs to the Greek Orthodox Church and that this testimony is in line with the central message of this book that the "divine bud" can flourish within all of us irrespective of the official religions we profess.

I must also confess that I was deeply touched by the message that Georgina's classmates wrote about her and that they insisted that they would read during the mass that was said on her behalf on June 7, 2009. Again, it is the kind of message that adolescents can write if they are really convinced that their friend was such a special person, in my own words, a saint. Here is the message.

The Lord said: "let the little children come to me." Lord, you are our creator, our Father and our brother. Lord, we know that when you do something, it is for our own good. Lord, today we are mourning our sister, friend, daughter and classmate Georgina who has left us on May 28, 2009 during her surgical operation that she had been waiting for, eight years till today. It is written that when you take a precious being, you do it in order to give us several others and open doors to happiness. Lord, soothe our hearts with your love which is so soft, so pure and so true, my God. His goodness towards us is so great and his faithfulness lasts everlastingly. Ps. 117-2. Lord, you do not forget any of your children. We know it. Soothe her family and fill them with much energy to enable them to bear this profound suffering because they really need it at this moment of great pain.

Lord, we ask you in our state of poor sinners, while imploring you to forgive us our sins because your beloved son died crucified on that cross for us. Lord, we praise you everlastingly. Amen.

Let my mouth proclaim the praise of the Eternal and that all flesh bless His holy name, for ever and ever (Ps. 145-21). Lord, send your angels in order to lead us and to show us the path that leads to you. He restores my soul, he leads me through the paths of justice and because of his name, when I walk in the valley of the shadow of death, I am not afraid of any evil because you are with me Ps. 23-334. May your soul rest in peace near the almighty Lord!

Georgina, we will always love you and may your soul rest in peace and quiet near our Lord Almighty, our God and His beloved Son Jesus Christ, Amen. (There is a heart drawing at the end of the written message.

As I read these passages, I still regret that Georgina has departed. I have always heard that when someone is about to die in a family, people will always sense it. In the traditional beliefs of people of my ethnic community, one usually knows it through tremors of the eyebrows. It is curious that none of us, that is, Jacky and I as Georgina's parents did not experiment them. If we had experimented them, maybe, we could have had second thoughts about the decision to send Georgina to Ghana for that operation. But we so trusted God that we never envisaged her possible death. Like I have said earlier, I knew that she would have to suffer temporarily during her convalescence, and this would still be very hard on me because I thought I would be feeling her physical pains as psychological pains in my body. But we knew that God was with us and that he would sustain us during the whole ordeal. As she is now dead, Jacky was nonetheless warned in a special way that Georgina was dying. She said that, when the doctor called her, she was reading this Biblical passage:

"Lord, you have been our dwelling place throughout all generations. Before the mountains were born or you brought forth the earth and the world, from everlasting to everlasting you are God. You turn men back to dust, saying, "return to dust, o souls of men." (Psalm 90:1-3)

All our days pass away under your wrath; we finish our years with a moan. The length of our days is seventy years— or eighty, if we have the strength; yet their span is but trouble and sorrow, for they quickly pass, and we fly away. Who knows the power of your anger? For your wrath is as great as the fear that is due you. Teach us to number our days aright, that we may gain a heart of wisdom." Psalm 90:9-12)

As I now think about it, I can see clearly that it is a passage that literally concerned Georgina. Yes, God told you: "return to dust," and the "Lord is your dwelling place throughout all generations." Note that Jackie was reading the passage in the French version of the Bible and the expression "for they quickly pass, and we fly away" is translated in French as "life goes by quickly and we fly towards death [la vie passe vite et nous volons vers la mort]".

Georgina, now that you are permanently with the Lord in heaven, we just want to tell you that we have typed your very last manuscript message that you addressed to your brother and sister and that you wrote on the eve of your operation in Ghana. It is a message that will remain with us and from which, hopefully, other people will benefit as they read it or read this book. This is the message:

A message from Georgine Mutaka

This is a note that Georgina wrote to Nadine and Eric in the evening of May 27 while in Ghana. She was going to get operated on the 28th by Dr Adjei Boachie of Focos. In a sense, this is a goodbye message because, on the 28th of May, 2009, she was traveling for eternity. We believe firmly that she is still watching over us as she has been called back to our Lord. To us, she is now a saint. She died while she was so close to our Lord. I still remember her evening prayers on the eve of the day she and Jackie left for Ghana. Nadine, Jackie, and Georgina prayed in Georgina and Nadine's room. All of them stressed the fact that God had at last heeded our prayers.

From: Georgine
To: Nadine and Eric
{keep this note until I'm back so that I can laugh}

I just want to tell you guys to be generous and helpful to each other.

Even if I am here [in Ghana], I'm stil1l seeing you. Watch out!!!

Laugh.
Small drawing of a smiling face. My eyes.

You have to stay and play with Collette, Valois, etc.

Please, keep praying for me and not crying for me.

I'm just going to have what you know and it's GOD that answered our prayers; so you should be grateful and joyful.

Please, study well, love one another [yourselves], and work (chores) well. When I come back, I want to see you as

141

secondary school children. I made all my best to teach you Maths, English, French, and General Paper.

Please Eric, stop this nonsense that you usually do and Nadine, be helpful.

> Be happy as I am. I'll see you soon.
> Perfume for you
> I love you guys.
> Georgine

As we read this message, we probably do not find anything extraordinary about it. It is the message that an elder sister would simply write to her junior brother and sister so as to encourage them to work hard. Yes, Georgina was smart at school. She knew that her sister was also smart, that is why she does not give her any special admonitions. But she was aware that her brother needed to work harder.

Where I would like to draw the reader's attention is the mention of Colette and Valois in the message. These were neighbors. Colette was about her age and Valois was a seven-month toddler. He was born here in Yaounde from Rwandan refugee parents.

I wonder if these two words, "Rwandan refugee," ring any bell in your mind. They may not ring a bell for many people. But for those who have met the Rwandan refugees, they are likely to have mixed feelings about them. Some came here to Cameroon because they were rich. Most of those refugees have actually gone to Europe, some to Canada and others to Australia. Those who are still here are the ones who have not found the means to also leave this country.

What links the central theme of this book to the Rwandan refugee case is this idea of the existence of God. Does God really exist? If he exists, why did he permit Rwandans to allow massive massacres of the Hutu and Tutsi, all of them actually daughters of their country, Rwanda? When we hear about those massacres, we take it as something quite normal because we have been accustomed to the idea that there was a massacre of the Tutsi in Rwanda. At times, we are likely to consider the Hutu that we see here in Cameroon as the genocide perpetrators. Unfortunately, this is all wrong. Most of them are victims.

This is an opportunity to remind the reader that God knew that this massacre would take place. I remember that it must have been in the year 1982 or 1983. At that time, I was living in Bukavu, DRC. We learned that the Holy Virgin was making regular appearances at Kibeho in Rwanda. She used to appear to two children. I do not remember the details, but I know about it because I had a colleague teacher who had a crippled child. His wife had already visited several hospitals and she thought that the Holy Virgin might operate a miracle on her child. She never did, at least for that specific child. What is interesting, however, is that the main message of the Holy Virgin was to invite the Rwandans to make peace among themselves, to repent and to seek the protection of the Lord. Otherwise, she insisted, a great catastrophe was going to befall on the Rwandan people.

At that time, no one believed that prophecy. There was no war in Rwanda. In fact, I know that many Congolese used to go and work in Rwanda because the living conditions were far better there than they were in the DRC. This massive massacre that occurred in 1994 must have been the one that the Holy Virgin came to warn people about.

If you were to read about the atrocities that were committed in Rwanda, you will always thank your God to have given you the privilege of not being in Rwanda at that time. From the testimonies that I read on internet from a certain Abdul who actually lives in Norway, both Hutu and Tutsi were trapped in their own country. I personally do not doubt Abdul's testimony because he states that he was part of the APR army and he mentions so many places and so many people that he cannot have been making them up. Just to recount some of the facts, he says that the Tutsi inside Rwanda were not much valued by the APR army that attacked from Uganda. In fact, some of the Tutsi were killed on purpose so that the government of Habyarimana may be accused of genocide. They never accepted journalists to report on their actions. Before attacking a given village, they would surround it, and when people would try to flee, that is, by hurriedly leaving the village in order to hide in the bush, they would then encounter the APR soldiers and get killed. He describes in details the different ways people were killed.

Again, it is difficult to imagine that he was lying because he was describing something that he saw his APR colleagues doing. He accepted to publish his identity and his email address in case people wanted to check on him. The following are the addresses given in the document in case some readers want to check the source of these excerpts.

The name of the author: Lt. Abdul Ruzibiza
Address: Birkeneveien 62
4647 Brennâsen
Norwegia
Email: ruzibiza@operamail.com
Name of the translators: AVICA7asbl
Email address of the translators: avica@tiscali
The address of the translators of the document:

BP. 33 Grand Place
1348 Louvain-La-Neuve

To give you a feel of the atrocities that might be read in that document, let me just give a few excerpts here. The document was originally written in Kinyarwanda and the version that I read and that appeared on internet is in French. The date appearing in the document for its elaboration is April 7, 2004. The following are therefore my translations.

Commenting on the way crimes were made as a trial to test the strategy of the APR to disrupt the Rwandan government, one can read the following:

"The FPR made trials in its intoxication strategy that consisted of making crimes that they would then attribute to the MRND in a bid to see what the results would look like."

As for the criteria used for selecting the people who got killed, I just want to let you read the following excerpts to make you realize that, if you were in Rwanda at that time, you could have been a victim. These people who died were innocent victims and we need to pose an act to help establish the kingdom of God here on earth, to do God's will so that such atrocities never happen again.

"People were killed to find accusations against the MRND, whether they had offended them or not. For those murders, the FPR used technicians (of the Network) or an extended branch among the agents of information of units and small squadrons of death; it also used some young people to whom they had taught the use of small bombs throughout the country. The selection of the people who had to be eliminated was made following these criteria:

1. Any Hutu who worked with good intentions for the Government, in other words, any Hutu who liked Habyarimana and his government;

2. Any Hutu who showed evidence to be intelligent and obstinate such as Gapyisi ;

3. Any Hutu who was an opponent and whose death could easily be attributed to the government;

4. Any Hutu whose death would not leave traces for subsequent inquiries;

5. Any military official, preferably, high-ranking;

6. No Tutsi born in Rwanda could be trusted; his death could easily be attributed to the government and was thus not considered a loss (it was normal to sacrifice the Tutsi living in Rwanda);

7. Any intellectual Tutsi who would not accept to embrace the FPR ideology, for example, Lando that we tried to kill on several occasions but kept missing;

8. The Tutsi who dwelled in isolated locations could easily be massacred as a group and their murder would thus be attributed to the MNRD. The soldiers of the FPR accomplished this type of mass murder in Kabatwa at Gisenyi, under the commandment of Gashayija Bagirigomwa as well as the information agent, Moses Rubimbura. These are not rumors. This kind of behavior also took place at the beginning of 1994.

9. Even after the war, the FPR did not hesitate to sacrifice the Tutsi in a bid to find pretexts to pillage the wealth of Zaire. It is no secret for any of the soldiers of FPR-Inkotanyi that the massacres of the Bagogwe of Mudende were perpetrated; we are able to supply proofs to whoever wants

146

them, the massacres of the Banyamulenge of Biura and of other localities were perpetrated from a similar mindset."

I just want to also mention some of the techniques the APR used to kill people as I was told that one of the techniques of using sexual relations between close relatives was used in Butembo, that is, Georgina's parents' native city in the DRC.

"To get information from an individual, it was necessary to torture him and kill him progressively: stabbing him with a knife several times, burning him with drops of heated plastic, pinching his genitals with needles, --compelling the brothers and sisters to have sexual relations, or a daughter to have sexual relations with her father or a son to have sexual relations with his mother even though the torturers have been duly informed that the people who were thus being tortured were close relatives..."

As one reads about the atrocities committed during the genocide, one cannot help thinking that the perpetrators had a purely satanic behavior while killing people. Consider for example this excerpt:

"The Tutsi of the FPR, I mean the military, have committed mass murder of the Hutu, in great numbers. To be more specific, the Tutsi of the FPR have killed any Hutu that they met or any Hutu that they happen to get an opportunity to kill. This despicable crime has been committed by around 23000 military people of the FPR. Some did it because it was an order given by the chief; others did it by sheer pleasure of killing, and all that because it was a right, an

147

authorization that came from a single man: (for security reasons, I do not write his name. See the original document)."

One should also bear in mind that, even among the APR soldiers, there were good people who also became victims of their chiefs and they were led to kill their own people. This is shown from the following excerpt:

"As days went on, some of the recruits among the Inkotanyi came from Rwanda in large numbers. Apart from those who came from Uganda who pretended that there were no real Tutsi inside Rwanda, and that those who had stayed there were materialist, that they did not want to go to exile, and that they were in fact Hutu in their way of thinking, as for us who originated from Rwanda, we were determined to go and help our families who were being decimated. What is really surprising and pushed a number of our own companions to commit suicide is that they prevented us from saving people who were dying as we saw them with our own eyes. Some took their weapons to commit suicide while declaring that they had made a mistake by getting enrolled willingly as Inkotanyi."

I really do not know how this genocide could have been averted. I also know that the Rwandan government still exhibits the skulls of the people who got massacred in this war so that people may not forget it. Only one side has been accused. The APR has not been made responsible. It is not that I want to render them responsible. I know that a lot of Rwandan survivors have found in their hearts the need to forgive. This is very positive. I know that they are being encouraged by their president. I wish that, if the present authorities know that they played some role in this massacre, that they also publicly confess it. They can be sure that they will be forgiven. Maybe, this will be a way for God to show that he can forgive any crime if you ask for that forgiveness. In the case of our Rwandan leaders, they have the power and this would make the very best sensation if, suddenly, they can confess some of their wrongdoings, give details about what they did and ask for forgiveness. They will continue to be the leaders of Rwanda. Hopefully, they will help end this rivalry that exists among the different ethnic groups. As they know, their rivalry has had ineffable consequences in the DRC. People talk about 4 million people who have been massacred. This makes four times the number of people who were massacred in Rwanda. And what is strange about this is that people tend to forget about this massacre of the 4 million people in eastern DRC. The only massacres that people remember are the ones in Rwanda.

If we do not repent, our God will have to ask us to account for our responsibility in those massacres. What if we repent and we recognize our responsibility and then work for peace to make sure that such massacres will never happen again. Would not this be the greatest lesson we would have learned from this war in Rwanda? That would indeed be the nicest dream, the one that we always recite in the Lord's prayer, notably "thy kingdom come, thy will be done on earth as it is in heaven". I solemnly invite our Rwandan authorities to make this contribution. I wish I had a way to tell them that they will be forgiven and that, like Paul who used to persecute the Christians and who later on became the staunchest defender of the Christian faith, they too will be playing this role of working for real peace in this part of the world. I know that they can do it if they want.

Now that we have pictured the Rwandan genocide, and possibly the massacres in the DRC, it is time to really ponder what can help us avert any further catastrophes similar to these massacres. Georgina's death has been an opportunity for us to remember such cases. Maybe, her early demise was also in God's plan to reach millions of people so that they may get the opportunity to hear this message of re-awakening the "divine bud" in all of us so that we might live in a better world. Once we accept this idea of the "divine bud," we can then afford to discuss more controversial topics and hopefully adopt solutions that are consonant with God's will and that are beneficial to us.

Indeed, if readers from all walks of life, belonging to various faiths can read this book with the idea that we are treating these controversial topics from the point of view of a child who has been called back to God, who is a friend of God, who does tell us that, if we can accept to become again like little children, as Jesus wanted us to be, we will be able to be much closer to him. Maybe, there are so many problems that we will be able to solve. We will be working on the great commission that he planned for us, notably, that "thy will be done on earth as it is in heaven." As you very well know, God's will does not stand a chance of being fulfilled if we, human beings, do not take a step of turning it into reality. Christians all over the world may recite or sing millions and millions of "our father who art in heaven" with that wish "thy will be done on earth as it is in heaven," if they cannot think about their personal involvement of working on its realization, then I declare that we are all hypocrites because nothing will ever be done. As you read this passage, why don't you take a look at your own life and decide to commit your life in working towards the realization of that wish? This will not disrupt your life; on the contrary, it will even give a worthwhile meaning to it if you can consider your lifetime here on earth as merely a passage to your own spiritual life after your death.

The first topic I wish us to discuss concerns extremism in religion. No child, whatever religion he belongs to, can be an extremist. Extremism is something that is learned. It cannot be innate. It is something that develops from the daily frustrations of grownups, not children, who see a lot of injustice and that they attribute to a category of people. These adults then influence their children who then grow up in this atmosphere of suspicion.

As for fighting any seeds of extremism among Catholics and Protestants, why don't you bear in mind that, adopting the attitude of retaining the divine bud in what all of us believe, you will still remain pretty the same people with most of your heartfelt beliefs. But we can fight our differences if we retain the fundamental message from Jesus. Love God above everything and love your neighbor as you love yourself. I suspect that priests and the whole clergy are the ones who grow the seeds of suspicion among their flocks in order for them to distrust Protestants. If you truly think about your private lives, would you really say that you are the representatives of God here on earth? Would you really say that you are much closer to God than some of your lay Christians or some of the Protestant Christians? You jolly well know that you are not, when you consider your private lives. As your flocks, we do see the way you behave. At times, you will see a bishop who, at night, is sometimes found with a lover. He forgets that people see him. I certainly know a number of bishops who have children. One of the archbishops in the DRC was finally asked to retire. Another archbishop easily accepted his child whenever he came to visit him. Another bishop, when he was finally told that his life is a scandal, he became so furious that he decided to send away the priest who dared tell him that he is no longer keeping the straight path that God traced for his flock, especially the priests and the bishop. These are bishops or priests who have complete faith in the Virgin Mary. I hope that, in the name of the divine bud that is in all of us and that manifests itself through children, they accept to become children again, in the eyes of the Lord, and repent themselves. I pray that they also make peace with their subordinates who took the courage of telling them that they were in the wrong path. Believe me, we all make mistakes. Our Lord will forgive you. He has forgiven David. You too, he will forgive you and he will let you pursue doing his divine work with a more peaceful heart. At the end of your earthly life, you will know that God will receive you as those little children that he receives. You know that, whoever you are, a Pope, a bishop, a priest, a cardinal, when you die and when you present yourself before your God, you are a child. God will not be awed by your presence because you were feared by human beings in your earthly existence.

Let us now tackle the issue of Muslim extremism. This message is particularly addressed to the Talibans. They say that they are the disciples of God. We accept that. Let us try to see this discipleship under the perspective of the divine bud. If you are true Talibans, you will not want to be killing people in the name of God. A child does not kill people that way. There is no justification for such an act. Most of your actions, you know that you do them because there is hatred in your hearts. You probably hate these Americans because they have been exploiting your raw materials. You hate these imperialists because they believe that they have to impose their way of thinking onto the whole world. You want to prove to them that you will not accept it. However, think about it. Are you becoming a kamikaze on your own will? Tell the truth. Isn't it because you are obliged to do so by a brother of yours who is a Taliban and who has this beard. He probably has promised money to your family. He has promised you that, upon your death, you will directly go to heaven. Don't you believe that you have made him your God? You know that God is so indefinable. You cannot capture him by saying that what a given Taliban has told me, or a given pastor has told me, is what God is. The whole point of this book is to show that God has manifested himself through all sorts of people who do not share necessarily your faith. God is certainly not Muslim. He is not Catholic. He is not Buddhist. At the same time, there is this divine bud that is in all these faiths. What if we were to espouse our faith with the mind and the eyes of little children? Are you truly going to impose to a child (the adult that you actually are) to go and kill people because they happen not to practice the same religion as yours? Is it really God who wants you to impose yourselves on women and ask them to stay at home, not to receive any education? You will not want to do it to little children who are the epitome of the divine bud. They are innocent. They need to continue growing as divine buds until they become adults.

To help you question your blind commitment to what your hierarchical authorities tell you that you will go to God's paradise when you die as a Kamikaze, consider this. Did you ever wonder if these authorities are willing to die as Kamikaze themselves? How come that the source of their money is mostly linked to drug trafficking? Is it also God's will that they be the ones to control this drug trafficking? I certainly do not know what happens to your soul when you die as a Kamikaze. I will never know. But I doubt that your place will be near God that we universally worship. He is a God of justice and peace. Not a God who wants his children to be dying as kamikaze by killing a lot of other innocent people and thus shattering other people's lives. If you cannot receive this message from me, as you read this book, could you at least seek a response to your behavior from your own Koran? Does the Koran tell you to kill people and sacrifice yourself as a Kamikaze? I do not know the answer. But, since the Muslims always tell us that they accept God's message through the Ancient Testament of the Bible, I am pretty sure that the God of this Ancient Testament, who is presumably therefore the God of the Koran, never has this in his plan of selecting Kamikaze as the people who will dwell in his paradise as his close friends.

Let us also ponder this issue related to the relationship between Muslims and the Christians: what if we really have the same God! What if Mohammed confirmed what is in the Bible, including the arrival of Jesus Christ of the Gospels! If we really behave like little children, Muslims and Christians, we will realize that we are not that different. There is this divine bud in all of us. Maybe the differences will remain as long as we genuinely believe in the value of our respective religions. But let us be ready to seek God's guidance. If I am Christian and I genuinely feel that God wants me to become Muslim, let me become Muslim. And if I am a Muslim, and that God wants me to become Christian, let me become Christian. Our political and religious authorities should help us worship God in the religion that is truly closer to our aspirations. Most probably, many young people in the Arab countries would wish to serve God in a way that matches their integration in the modern world. They certainly do not want to worship the type of God that the Talibans would impose with the attendant consequences that a woman cannot drive, a woman cannot walk by herself without a man accompanying her, and a woman has to wear a black veil in public. If these religious authorities truly serve God, let them allow their followers to enjoy the freedom of practicing the religion of their own choice. Religion is not something that should be imposed. It is a relationship that, as an individual, you have with your God. It is true that you practice better your religion with other believers. But deep down in us, religion remains personal. The day you will die, you will be alone to face your God. Just as when you were born, you were alone. Each individual is unique. God wanted it that way. It would be nice that the society only helps us bloom the divine bud in all of us. If we can do it through our own religions, we will be accomplishing the will of God on earth.

Actually, if you think about it, on several occasions, Jesus told the people he healed through miracles that "your faith has saved you". Faith is something personal. It is also deeply ingrained in us and only God sees true faith in us. We cannot lie to Him. It does not matter which religion you belong to. God will save you when you implore Him with deep faith and he will also tell you: your faith has saved you. (I suspect that this might not be the official position of theologians, but it sounds right to me as I believe that God does care about every human being, not just Catholics or Protestants.)

Being a believer is not something easy. I do not want to give the impression that God always answers our prayers. You and I know that he does not. Every time, I always think about Job in the Bible and I pray that God never tests me as he tested Job. Being a divine bud is accepting also that God may not answer our prayer. When he does that, he is probably giving us a different message. As his creatures, we have got to do what is right. He is God. Upon our death, he will ask us if we did what he expected of us. Who are we to tell him if he fulfilled his part of the contract as encrypted in the biblical statement: ask and it will be given to you; seek and you will find; knock and the door will be opened to you (Matthew 7:7)! For many people, God has indeed accomplished that. But, maybe, in your own life, he did not do that. In the case of Georgina, he certainly decided to call her to him when she was going to celebrate her recovery as the direct answer to our prayers. We cannot be angry at God. Even if we happen to be swept away by natural catastrophes such as earthquakes, tsunamis, typhoons as has recently happened in Southeast Asia, we cannot condemn God. It is interesting to hear the survivors in such natural catastrophes always thanking God for saving their lives. They never condemn him and they are right. God is God and we will never reduce him into what we want him to be. But he expects us to behave according to his will. This is also part of what it means to maintain the torchlight on the divine bud inside us.

I wish I had a miracle to tell you about God's intervention in my own life. I have a good friend of mine who is a pastor. During his youth, he became an officer in the Cameroonian army. He was a colonel. He used to be close to the first president as he was his private pilot. If you see him today, you will never believe that he was a pilot. He had a very active life that I will not disclose because, if I did so, I would be revealing secrets about him that he never told me about himself but that I know very well. What I really want to tell you about him is that he became a pastor. He even got the power of being able to chase demons. At the same time, he had a personal life that was still linked to politics. Unfortunately, he became seriously ill. He has told me several times that he has been on the brink of death. I personally believe that it has been through our prayers that he always succeeded to survive. As I am writing these lines, he has a sore on his leg that prevents him from walking. It is really very painful. My own prayer to the Lord God has always been that God cures him from that sore and I have been asking the Lord God that he allows me to go and tell him that God has decided to heal his wound. So far, God has not heeded my prayers. I have been wondering whether there is a message that he is conveying to this pastor friend of mine for areas of his life that he led in the past. Again, God's ways are unfathomable by human beings. This pastor and I know that if he were to regain his full health, he will be very useful in a project that we have for finding means to get people to invite God in their lives. It is a project that requires a lot of money. With his connections, he knows the specific individuals he would have to contact to obtain money for this project as he had already talked to them in the past. It is a project that needs some follow-up and he is the only one to do that. Not even his wife or one of his sons who is a medical doctor can help us in this project. As I am writing these lines, I still hope that the Lord God will have pity on him and make him recover. To me, the promise that this pastor made to help me obtain funding for a project that would make the Lord better known by millions of sub-Saharan African people, if our project is successful, I consider that it is a promise that he made to God himself. He cannot betray this promise. And that is something hard but at the same time more enticing.

Making a promise to your creator is definitely much more binding. As you read the present document, our aim, that is, I and the sociolinguistics students who contributed testimonies of God's intervention we are publishing in the present document, is that you also make such promises to your God in order to contribute to the blooming of the divine bud inside you and in other people your exemplary behavior is likely to impact. Such a promise will definitely be a decisive step to put into practice the wish in the Lord's prayer, that is, "thy will be done as it is in heaven." As I said before, the advantage of such a pledge to your God, whatever religion you practice, will be to promote *"life which is indeed beautiful and which can be lived with joy and courage under all circumstances"* as Britta wrote, commenting on the passing away of Georgina. I wish to add a word of caution here. Although I include in this book this quotation from Britta's message, I am not suggesting that Christians should start integrating the teachings of Buddhism in their daily lives. As I see it, their magical chant, "Nam-myoho-renge-kyo" that they consider as "the ultimate law of the true aspect of life permeating all phenomena in the universe" (see San Gaudioso and Greg Martin 2007:303 in their book *The Buddha next door*), does not match up with the Lord's prayer (i.e., "Our Father") as it looks to me the perfect prayer I have ever been taught.

Chapter 9

Learning From Witnesses of the Divine Bud

By way of ending this novel, let me try to relate it to your own life. It is true that Georgina's death has prompted us to write it. However, I know that every single person among you has had a relative who has also died. For those whose children have perhaps passed away, my hope is that they will find some consolation in also believing that they died as angels and that they are with God. You also know a lot of people that you might not think of as potential angels because they were mean here on earth. Would you want to be remembered as an angel or as a cruel person whose death is welcomed by the people over whom you ruled? You know that, whoever you are, whatever power you might wield, you will just turn into dust, and your soul will survive in the world beyond where it will most probably have to face a divine judgment in order to account for your actions on earth. Why don't you take a personal decision to amend your deeds in order to attract a more favorable look from your divine judge? What does this mean?

The correct answer that comes into my mind is a passage that I wrote and published in a paper entitled "Growing seeds of peace in an African war-torn world" in Mutaka (ed.) *Building Capacity: using TEFL and African languages as development-oriented literacy tools*, 2008, Langaa Research and Publishing CIG, Mankon (printed in UK by Lightning Source UK Ltd), pp. 156-159. It is a long passage. I will paste some excerpts here and will be adding a few comments between parentheses after each excerpt.

-You are responsible of an institution and you manage public funds intended for example to fight AIDS in your country. However, because of your egotistical interests, you create artificial problems for allocating such funds unless the users find a way to pay you personally for the public service you are supposed to render. (I still believe this is true as I came to understand that many of the individuals who manage AIDS funds do not wish AIDS to be overcome because they would lose the source of their funding. There is this book, *Wish I had known / Si je savais,* that I wrote with my sociolinguistics students and colleagues as AIDS prevention material. Although the book is really excellent and that I was promised substantial government funding, I have never succeeded to obtain it simply because I have realized that one can never trust the authorities who manage these funds. The former prime minister who promised us funding was a truly godly person and he was doing his job in utmost honesty; after his removal, the promise has fizzled out for various reasons I myself cannot understand. The government did grant us limited funding for the printing of the English version of the book. Hopefully, the second edition of the book will be published outside Cameroon and more people will get a chance to have access to it.)

-You rape girls in the presence of their parents because your chief asked you to do so to humiliate these parents. And yet, you should know that God will ask you to account for such rapes at your death. But you ignore this internal call in order to satisfy your chief. (I wrote this in reaction to what I learned when I visited my country in 2002. Rape as a crime is unfortunately used by many evildoers in several parts of the world. I hope the rapists heed this message.)

-You decide to bomb the "twin towers" in New York City, as a way to play a dirty trick to these Americans, by using their own planes, just because you have been told that, were you to die as a "kamikaze" in such a bombing, you will go to paradise. You never ask yourself this question: what kind of God will tell me that I deserve to go to paradise because I have succeeded to shatter and destroy the lives of many individuals, including Muslim individuals like yourself? What about the ineffable misfortune that the families of the victims of such bombings will undergo? Will your God see this as the best way for you to enter paradise and will God view the shattering of the other individuals' lives as irrelevant because your life is far more important than anybody else's? We hope you know that this is not the God you really believe in. It is certainly not the God who will ask you to account for your earthly life upon your death in order to decide which group of people you should join in the after-life world. (One year earlier before the twin towers were destroyed, an American family, more precisely Rachel and her mother, made me visit one of the twin towers. It was my most memorable visit of New York City. It is so sad that future generations will no longer experience the feeling of watching the roads of New York City from the 110th floor as I did then.)

-You are a civil servant and you attribute yourself huge amounts of money by creating government-paid fake missions. You belong to the inner circle of government people who get huge salaries in a country where people live in abject conditions because of public funds mismanagement. A clear case will better illustrate this. One civil servant from a francophone African country told us that, a PDG (i.e. a government company director) gets 750 US dollars daily when he goes on mission. If he chooses to travel with any member of his family, his wife gets 350 US dollars and each child gets 150 US dollars. The hotel bill as well as the food will still be paid by the government company. There are also other government companies where the members are paid 1000 US dollars for merely participating at the monthly meeting. Notice that the members of the government company he was talking about were not Africans only. There were Europeans among them. He ensured us that the information was true because he succeeded to become a member of one such government company. He also told us that, although he himself is not a PDG, he gets 500 US dollars daily when he goes on mission for his company. Note that this is a country where, officially, a University professor's monthly salary is about 100 US dollars. To survive, it seems that university professors oblige their students to pay their courses and if you do not pay the course, you will not get a grade from him. We wonder why foreign organizations such as the International Monetary Fund and the World Bank do not exert pressure on the leaders of such countries to take drastic measures that would render their finances more transparent and safe. We wish foreign individuals of good will whose countries have been pouring money in these countries under the guise of bilateral or multilateral cooperation to obtain reliable information on (a) the salaries of the ministers and other top government officials of such countries, (b) the system that allows them to siphon out money, for example through the organization of fake missions in foreign countries or the organization of conferences whose real motivation is to find a way of spending the money that the international organizations pour into their countries. Our bet is that they will realize that, to a certain extent, they have been contributing, unknowingly, to worsen the situation in these countries because they have never forcefully denounced the mismanagement of public funds to the right decision makers of their own countries likely to make things change in these African countries. (As a comment, soon after Barack Obama was elected president of the United States, an American friend of mine asked me to tell her what I wished the new American government to do in order to help my country and Africa in general as she said that there was a way to send the message to the president's team which helped elect him as president. What I did was to send her the paper from which these excerpts are taken. I hope President Barack Obama's team read the paper. I was happy to see that when the new American Secretary of State, Hilary Clinton, visited Kinshasa, she insisted on some of the suggestions I had given in the paper. I simply wish that more should be done by foreign rich governments to help our African leaders be far more responsible in the way they manage government funds as suggested in this excerpt.)

-Circumstances have conspired to make of you the president or an elected official of your country. You are fully aware of man-made causes of poverty in your country. Most often, your closest collaborators are the ones who ruin the country because of the deep-ingrained practices of corruption. You condone their actions and do not take any steps to straighten up the situation. And yet, you still ask people's votes and you make them believe that you are the best choice of the Christians or the Muslims in your country. You make sure that your people regularly see you at church or in the mosques. Our wish is that your conscience tells you to act less hypocritically and serve the people who put you in that office because, soon or later, you will have to account for your actions upon your death.

-You are the president of the most powerful nation on earth. You know that you can exert a decisive influence on the leaders of some African countries not to perpetuate evil on their neighbors. But you choose not to do it because you believe this will not have any bearing to your own re-election. Worse still, you choose to ignore the evidence that tells you that some of these leaders you support are using the money you give their countries to kill their own populations or their neighbors. And yet, you make everybody believe that you are a very sincere Christian. The Pope is your friend. You make sure that, before you stage a war on a given country, your soldiers seek the protection of your God in order to win the war. We hope that, somewhere, this God will tell your conscience to also act in the best interest of the numerous people who feel weak and hope that your intervention in their African countries, may help alleviate some of the evils they feel are being perpetrated against them. (While this remains true, I wish to say that this definitely does not apply to President Barack Obama. I wrote it before he became president. It is curious that he has even been awarded the Nobel Peace prize for this year 2009. This is certainly a strong message to him to work for peace, and hopefully to look again at the suggestions I gave in the paragraph above where I mentioned his name that he should insist that our African governments do not mismanage the funds earmarked for fighting poverty in our countries.)

-You are the Secretary General of the UN. You know that you can ask the leaders of the nations to take a decisive action to punish the people who commit rapes as a war tool. And yet, you do not do anything because there are more urgent issues you are dealing with in New York City. One might even wonder what your real priorities are. Is it to allow various leaders and organizations to siphon out the UN money by organizing conferences, paying very high hotel bills to the organizers, or very high salaries to your own staff in various countries as if you are mocking the workers in those countries that what they do for the benefit of their people is not as important as what your UN staff does in those countries? And you do nothing for these girls who are raped, for these millions of people who are displaced from their land because of a war that has been staged by some of your friends who sit in the UN and with whom you sip peacefully your champagne while these hundreds of millions of people are being killed. We hope that we can all wake up and know that we should perhaps do more justice in this world, just to make sure that our own judge will not tell us that we abused the power he so gracefully bestowed upon us. (Note that this was written prior to the election of the current UN Secretary).

I also wish to say that Georgina's death has also helped me discover golden hearts in some people I would not have suspected that they possessed. When we always pray that 'thy kingdom come, thy will be done on earth as it is in heaven," I truly think that if people were to behave like those who wrote the following email messages I will presently share with you, the world would be a paradise.

The first message is from Francisca Adjei. This is a teacher that I met in Ghana. She was very simple. It is true that, what I remember about her is that we probably liked each other without expressing it verbally. I had no reason to really interact with her. But she somehow remarked my presence and offered to sometimes get food for me at the cafeteria because I was not aggressive enough to serve myself in the middle of many conference participants. As I returned to Cameroon, I told Jackie about her that I found her very sympathetic and that I was sure she will accept to host Georgina when we will send her to Ghana for the operation.

When we first established contact with the Focos team for Georgina's surgical operation, we were asked to send Georgina to Ghana unaccompanied. At that time, Jackie was in my home country, visiting her sick mother. When I contacted Francisca, she accepted wholeheartedly that she will host Georgina. She simply inquired whether she can speak English, and I said yes. She is the one who gave us the initial information about the conditions for the operation. You remember that they told us at first that it would cost us around 3 thousand dollars, then 5 thousand dollars, then between six and ten thousand dollars, then 25 thousand dollars when my daughter called the Focos team from the States. During this negotiation period, Georgina ended up not going to Ghana by herself. She finally went there with Jackie as I indicated at the beginning of this book. You already know the outcome, that is, Georgina's death.

For my wife, the ideal situation for her to live in Ghana was to rent an apartment where she would stay with Georgina. She likes to be independent. This turned out to be impossible and Francisca could not help. Although her family used to live in Accra, she and her husband had to leave Accra and go some 50 kms inland. Despite their good will to help us, they could not put up Georgina and Jackie. But I must emphasize that Francisca simply took Georgina as her own daughter. I will not be able to express this in words, but she really made me feel that she fully accepted Georgina. This is extraordinary. It is so nice that people can thus love strangers from the bottom of their hearts. I wish we could learn from her to also be ready to sometimes give a helping hand to our neighbor in time of need.

I have also treasured this message she expressed in the following email:

From: Francisca Adjei
To: pmutaka@yahoo.com (pmutaka@gmail.com)
Date: Tuesday, November 18, 2008 12:41:34 PM

High Prof

I must congratulate you for showing all the love to this child for 15 years. When problems come, (in my religion (Eckankar), we see problems as situations we have to master. Let us not ask God to take the problem away but rather ask Him what lessons we have to learn from the situation/problem. God will not give you what you cannot handle. There is always a way out. Trust the God within you. There's always help and it will come when necessary and the right time, for nothing can stop the hand of God

I have a niece called NUSINYO
NU SI NYO
thing which good
'that which is good'

According to one of my aunties who named this child looking at the circumstances surrounding her birth, "God only does what is good" meaning it is only the best that God will give you.

Cheer up. Greetings to the family.

She wrote this message almost seven months before Georgina would die. If you re-read it, you will find it very touching and true. In her case, I just wish to tell you that she and her husband became Jackie's close relatives in Ghana. As you remember, Arlette was able to join Jackie but I could not fly to Ghana for reasons that have to do with the disorganization of my country: I could not have a passport and could not thus travel to Ghana to bury my own daughter. As you know, in times of grief and great suffering, one needs a companion. Francisca became Jacky's closest companion in Ghana. As she has told me, many other Ghanaians, including members of the Focos team, also assisted her morally. They were for example able to organize a mass before they brought Georgina's remains to the cemetery. I will refrain from mentioning some other gifts that Francisca gave to Jackie. Her whole behavior was that of a woman who wanted to express her own sympathy through a unique way of showing Jackie that she very much loved Georgina as her own daughter. Thank you Francisca, and thank you all your friends like Ephraim Nsoh, the priest and other people like the members of the Focos team that only Jackie knows for having been so compassionate during her bereavement in Ghana.

The second message I wish to share with you comes from the parents of my daughter's fiancé. Yes, at that time, they were still fiancés. I wish to tell you that Josh, Arlette's fiancé, is American. I know that many people might wonder if there can really be true love between a white American and a black African. As I live in Cameroon, I know that Cameroonian girls usually seek a white husband because it would be the easiest way for them to go and live abroad, preferably in France or in other western countries. Many of them find their white husbands on Internet. This has not been the case for my daughter. It is true that she spent her early childhood in the States and went back to the States because she always remembered the country of her childhood. Her fiancé happens to be someone who had visited Africa and who had spent almost a year in the city where Arlette was born. This is Bukavu in eastern DRC. His present job still allows him to sometimes visit Africa. This is how he had met Georgina and knew in his heart that Georgina loved him. He had in fact spent a night on Georgina's own bed. You should now understand why he, just like Arlette, was so devastated when he learned Georgina's unexpected demise.

Again, the reason I am writing this is to show how gratifying it is to love other people. I would say that true love is contagious. True love cannot be mistaken. From the following email, I would like to share with you excerpts of the letter that Josh's parents addressed to us, that is, Jackie and me as Arlette's parents. The reason I am sharing it with you is to tell you that, to a certain extent, it is a prolongation of love for Georgina. Besides, I know that Georgina's death has somehow precipitated Josh's decision to make public and strengthen his relationship with Arlette and, ultimately, to create a strong binding between Josh and Arlette's two families. As you read these excerpts, you will realize that these lines were written from people who expressed true love from the bottom of their hearts. Read them first before I make a few useful comments.

To: Philip and Jackie Mutaka
From: Stephen P. Marks and Kathleen A. Modrowski
Date :   September 24, 2009
Re: Josh and Arlette

Dear Philip and Jackie,

Your warm and charming introduction to your kind family touched Kathleen and me very deeply.

Your daughter has brightened our lives while bringing so much happiness to Josh. During our Christmas holidays in Florida and her several visits to us in Southampton and our visits to Washington, we have come to know Arlette as a bright, caring, resourceful, and lovely person, whom we welcome into our family with open arms. Her qualities derive in no small part from her good fortune to be born into such a loving family, one that treasures family ties and education. We were all devastated by the loss of Georgina. We know how close Arlette was to her and devoted to her cure, which turned out so tragically. Kathleen and I join Joshua in sharing your grief.

From your description, Jane has had a positive influence on Arlette and knows her well. It is all the more gratifying to learn that our impressions of Arlette and Josh as a happy couple are confirmed by someone who knows her so well.

We are grateful for your very kind remarks about Josh and pleased that he has been accepted into your family. We have both traveled in Africa and have a deep appreciation for the culture and values of the diverse and wonderful peoples of Africa. You can imagine our satisfaction when Josh developed a whole-hearted commitment to Africa, both professionally and affectively. We are very proud of the depth of his knowledge of the politics, sociology, and languages of the region of Central Africa and rejoice in his deepening his personal involvement by sharing his life with such a magnificent daughter of Africa. Of course, I would be honored to conform to African tradition in an appropriate symbolic way which we can discuss. We share the objective of the happiness of our beloved children. [...]

You describe Jackie as very active and the best mother. We can see how much Arlette has benefited from such a role model.

Kathleen and I are, as you say, both involved in higher education. Her training is in cultural anthropology and she had the advantage of working with some of the leaders in her field in the various universities of Paris and of doing her field work in Tunisia. My training is in international law and relations, which I have been able to practice in various roles for UNESCO, the Ford Foundation, the UN, and to teach, primarily at Princeton, Columbia and, for the past decade, at Harvard. Truth be told, we are--by experience and temperament--cosmopolitan, in the most positive connotation of the term. We both work in the field of human rights and are intellectually and militantly committed to protecting the dignity and promoting the flourishing of all members of the human family. As you know, Kathleen is currently director of Global Studies at Long Island University in New York and I direct a program on Human Rights in Development at the Harvard School of Public Health in Boston. We have just returned from an extended trip to India, for example, and hope to return there.

171

But our travels in the near future must bring us to Africa so that we can have the joy of making your acquaintance in person.

Kathleen and I both rejoice in knowing that Josh and Arlette will have their American and their African families and cultures, and welcome the bonds that will unite us all.

Thank you once again for your kind and thoughtful correspondence. We look forward to hearing more news and to meeting you in the future.

With warmest personal regards,

Steve and Kathleen

I believe what has really prompted me to publish this letter is that I view it as an implementation of the types of feelings I hoped to arouse in people who would read this novel I wrote and which is entitled *"the Fruit of Love."* One of the key ideas in the novel is that, in a marriage relationship, partners have to accept each other as the perfect gift of God. Let me just give you a quotation from the book that expresses it far better (Mutaka 2001:23):

"If we truly say that we believe in God, this means that we believe that God created Adam and Eve, and most importantly, that God created Eve as the best companion for Adam. Imagine a moment that you are before your creator, that you are Adam. You have been all alone. Among all the creatures in the world, there is not a single one that you find a "suitable helper" for you. You have been asleep. Then, as you wake up, you see Eve come to you. You are so delighted. God did not ask you what kind of wife you wanted to have. He just gave you Eve, with all her weaknesses and qualities. Adam accepted Eve. This is the way God has always wanted us to accept our wives.

Joey, Sarah is the Eve that God sent you. Keep that in mind. Sarah is the perfect gift that God chose for you. As a human being, she cannot be perfect. Her lack of perfection is part of what makes her a human being. If you can truly put into your mind that Sarah is the perfect gift that God provided for you, you will have a new vision of Sarah. You will trust Sarah. You know that Sarah needs your protection as her man."

The other idea from the novel is the necessity of promoting your partner's self-esteem. As said in the book, one guideline to build this self-esteem is to "help your mate experience the liberating power of unconditional love by accepting him or her completely." As a way to boost your mate's self-esteem, the following assignment is proposed in the novel (cf. Mutaka 2001:39):

"The words you speak to your mate have the potential to strengthen or poison your mate's self-esteem," according to Dennis and Barbara Rainey in their book "Building Your Mate's Self-Esteem." One sure way of boosting your partner's self esteem is to praise him/her. Can you help your partner know how to best appreciate you by telling him/her the following?

a. Are there any "weed seeds" you've planted in your mate's life for which you need to ask forgiveness?

b. What are some words, phrases, attitudes and actions which bring you down and discourage you?

c. What are some words, phrases, attitudes and actions that encourage you and lift your spirit?

As I read Josh's parents' letter, I was truly elated. I found that it contains the message that is likely to boost one's self-esteem. It reminded me of the feelings I used to have in the States as I felt completely accepted by the family of Sheri and Hank. As an African, I was raised with the strict respect of taboos. One such taboo was the sanctity of your host's bed. And yet, whenever this couple traveled, they would leave me in their house and they would ask me to be sleeping in their own bed and be using their own sheets and towels. And whenever they went to Sheri's parents, they would ask me to go with them to the extent that Sheri's parents' home became like my own. I really felt completely accepted and happy. I learned from that couple what it really means to love and feel loved. Another instance I even included in the *Fruit of Love* while talking about Sheri is that, I learned the benefits of spontaneous hugging between people in love. Sometimes, we would be standing in the middle of their living room, and then we would hug spontaneously. This hugging was also a sign of complete acceptance and love.

Jackie and I already knew Josh and we had accepted him completely. But we never heard directly from his parents, and we were not sure that they would accept Arlette wholeheartedly as she is black. This letter not only reassured us, but it also conveys a message of the American people to sub-Saharan Africans. You have read that they value our African cultures as well as the Africans. Arlette is merely a symbol of the Africans. To me, this is a message that is written by our American partners to Africans, and the individuals in the message are merely symbols. I am publishing it because I want you to feel that it is also particularly addressed to you. Josh's parents stand for our numerous benefactors from the developed countries who have been helping our countries because they sincerely like us as part of the human race.

As I work here in Cameroon, I have learned a lot from my sociolinguistics students about traditional marriage ceremonies. For example, among the Mvumbo of Cameroon, before the boy's family members would accept a girl, she is inspected carefully and she is tested about her capacity of supporting any kind of insults. I also know that, in many families, the mother-in-law or the sisters-in-law of the newlywed bride are often her enemies as they consider that she will be benefiting from the wealth that their son or brother might possess. I believe many Africans know that and they always manage to live with it. But it certainly does not contribute in building the self-esteem of the bride in her husband's family. In writing the *Fruit of Love*, I was hoping to arouse the new feeling of building one's partner's self-esteem as I believed that couples would feel happier when they know that they are completely accepted by their partner's families.

After reading the above letter, I did not air any of these feelings and was rather eager to print it and hand it to Jackie. I wanted to see how she would react to it. She too was extremely happy. In fact, she told me that I have to send it to Arlette as it is the kind of letter that will be encouraging her to maintain a stable family life. In other words, she immediately saw that it is a letter that would boost Arlette's self-esteem in her American family.

Why is all this important to you? Don't you want to be the conduit of God's love towards your neighbor? Because you know that, soon or later you will die, don't you want to change your life so as to be remembered as a person who was able to be a living symbol of the divine bud that is inside of us, no matter which religion we practice? As you ponder your own life, you may certainly find that you too have experimented the love that Francisca had for Georgina, that

175

is, love for a neighbor and that made her act as the best companion for Jackie during the bereavement period in Ghana. You will perhaps have a feeling that you could have written a letter much similar to Josh's parents' one as an expression of true love towards other people in your neighborhood, despite their race, culture, or religion. As you seek to make the divine bud flourish in you, this will enable you to view your neighbors with a more positive look. As I hinted earlier, maybe this might push the real perpetrators of the horrendous events of the Rwandan genocide or of the massacre of the four million people in eastern DRC to confess their evils and apologize because they know that the world will forgive them. To tell the truth, I do not expect them to openly confess it, but I imagine that they can encourage their citizens to be reading this present novel. This would be an indirect way to ask for forgiveness, and I am confident that they will be forgiven. In identifying yourself with the divine bud in you, you will be responding positively to God's plan for taking back Georgina's life as the trigger that would lead you to contribute to the accomplishment of this wish in the Lord's prayer, "thy will be done on earth as it is in heaven." AMEN.

www.ingramcontent.com/pod-product-compliance
Lightning Source LLC
Chambersburg PA
CBHW022318280326
41932CB00010B/1140